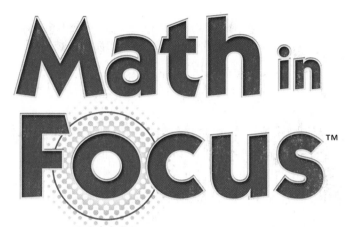

Math in Focus™

The Singapore Approach

Student Book

4A

Consultant and Author
Dr. Fong Ho Kheong

Authors
Chelvi Ramakrishnan and Gan Kee Soon

U.S. Consultants
Dr. Richard Bisk, Andy Clark,
and Patsy F. Kanter

Marshall Cavendish
Education

GREAT SOURCE®
HOUGHTON MIFFLIN HARCOURT
Supplemental Publishers

© 2009 Marshall Cavendish International (Singapore) Private Limited

Published by Marshall Cavendish Education
An imprint of Marshall Cavendish International (Singapore) Private Limited
A member of Times Publishing Limited

Marshall Cavendish International (Singapore) Private Limited
Times Centre, 1 New Industrial Road
Singapore 536196
Tel: +65 6411 0820
Fax: +65 6266 3677
E-mail: fps@sg.marshallcavendish.com
Website: www.marshallcavendish.com/education

Distributed by
Great Source
A division of Houghton Mifflin Harcourt Publishing Company
181 Ballardvale Street
P.O. Box 7050
Wilmington, MA 01887-7050
Tel: 1-800-289-4490
Website: www.greatsource.com

First published 2009
Reprinted 2010

Math in Focus ™ is a trademark of Times Publishing Limited.

Great Source ® is a registered trademark of Houghton Mifflin Harcourt Publishing Company.

Math in Focus Grade 4 Student Book A
ISBN 978-0-669-01084-8

Printed in United States of America

2 3 4 5 6 7 8   1897   16 15 14 13 12 11 10
4500219963   B C D E

Contents

1 Place Value of Whole Numbers

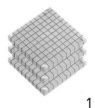

Learn Count on to ten thousand • Read and show numbers in
place-value charts • Count on to one hundred thousand• Find the value
of each digit in a number using a place-value chart • Find the
expanded form of a 5-digit number

Hands-On Activity Use play money to show 5-digit numbers
Game Find the Value!

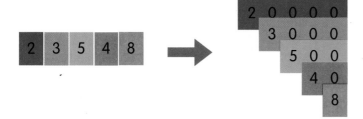

Look for **Practice and Problem Solving**

Student Book A and Student Book B	Workbook A and Workbook B
• **Let's Practice** in every lesson	• **Independent Practice** for every lesson

• Put on Your Thinking Cap!
  in every chapter
	• Put on Your Thinking Cap!
	  in every chapter

Ten Thousands	Thousands	Hundreds	Tens	Ones

Ten Thousands	Thousands	Hundreds	Tens	Ones
●				

10,000

Look for **Assessment Opportunities**

Student Book A and Student Book B	Workbook A and Workbook B
• **Quick Check** at the beginning of every chapter to assess chapter readiness	• **Cumulative Reviews** six times during the year
• **Guided Practice** after every example or two to assess readiness to continue lesson	• **Mid-Year and End-of-Year Reviews** to assess test readiness
• **Chapter Review/Test** in every chapter to review or test chapter material	

2 Estimation and Number Theory

Whole Number Multiplication and Division

Hundreds	Tens	Ones
$200 \times 3 = 600$	$30 \times 3 = 90$	$2 \times 3 = 6$

Tables and Line Graphs

5 Data and Probability

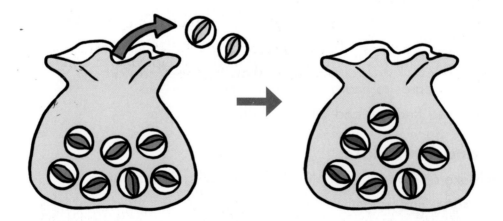

6 Fractions and Mixed Numbers

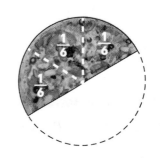

Welcome to

Math in Focus™

This exciting math program comes to you all the way from the country of Singapore. We are sure you will enjoy learning math with the interesting lessons you'll find in these books.

What makes *Math in Focus*™ different?

▶ **Two books** You don't write in the ____ in this textbook. This book has a matching **Workbook**. When you see the pencil icon 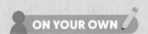 **ON YOUR OWN**, you will write in the **Workbook**.

▶ **Longer lessons** Some lessons may last more than a day, so you can really understand the math.

▶ **Math will make sense** Learn to use bar models to solve word problems with ease.

In this book, look for

Learn	**Guided Practice**	**Let's Practice**	**ON YOUR OWN**
This means you will learn something new.	Your teacher will help you try some sample problems.	You practice what you've learned to solve more problems. You can make sure you really understand.	Now you get to practice with lots of different problems in your own **Workbook**.

Also look forward to Games, Hands-On Activities, Math Journals, Let's Explore, and Put on Your Thinking Cap!

You will combine logical thinking with math skills and concepts to meet new problem-solving challenges. You will be talking math, thinking math, doing math, and even writing about doing math.

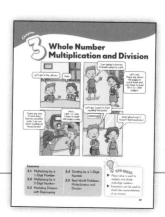

What's in the Workbook?

Math in Focus™ will give you time to learn important new concepts and skills and check your understanding. Then you will use the practice pages in the **Workbook** to try:

▶ Solving different problems to practice the new math concept you are learning. In the textbook, keep an eye open for this symbol **ON YOUR OWN** . That will tell you which pages to use for practice.

▶ *Put on Your Thinking Cap!*

Challenging Practice problems invite you to think in new ways to solve harder problems.

Problem Solving challenges you to use different strategies to solve problems.

▶ Math Journal activities ask you to think about thinking, and then write about that!

Students in Singapore have been using this kind of math program for many years.
Now you can too — are you ready?

Place Value of Whole Numbers

The distance around Earth is 24,092 miles.

Hmm, I wonder what the distances around the other planets are.

Lessons

BIG IDEA

▶ Read, compare, and order numbers according to the place value of their digits.

Recall Prior Knowledge

Writing numbers in three forms

Thousands	Hundreds	Tens	Ones

Word form: two thousand, three hundred seven
Standard form: 2,307
Expanded form: 2,000 + 300 + 7

Counting on by ones, tens, hundreds, or thousands

Count on by ones: 5,101   5,102   5,103   5,104 ...
Count on by tens: 2,001   2,011   2,021   2,031 ...
Count on by hundreds: 4,200   4,300   4,400   4,500 ...
Count on by thousands: 3,800   4,800   5,800   6,800 ...

Finding the value of each digit in a number

Thousands	Hundreds	Tens	Ones
4	7	2	8

stands for 4 thousands or 4,000	stands for 7 hundreds or 700	stands for 2 tens or 20	stands for 8 ones or 8

Comparing numbers using a place-value chart

	Thousands	Hundreds	Tens	Ones
2,910	2	9	1	0
2,688	2	6	8	8

First, compare the thousands. They are the same.
Then, compare the hundreds. 9 hundreds is greater than 6 hundreds.
So, 2,910 is greater than 2,688.

Completing a pattern by finding the rule

$$+ 200 \quad + 200$$
4,182   4,382   4,582   ?   4,982

Add 200 to 4,582 to get 4,782.
Check your answer by adding 200 to 4,782. You will get 4,982.
So, the rule is to add 200 to a number to get the next number in the pattern.

 Quick Check

Express each number in word form.

1 5,691

2 9,056

Express each number in standard form.

3 four thousand, one hundred nine

4 six thousand, twelve

Express each number in expanded form.

5 6,432 = ▢

6 3,805 = ▢

Continue each number pattern. Count on by ones, tens, hundreds, or thousands.

7 5,500   5,600   5,700   ▢

8 9,077   9,078   9,079   ▢

9 5,320   6,320   7,320   ▢

Complete.

In 5,628,

10 The digit 6 is in the ▢ place.

11 The value of the digit 5 is ▢.

12 The digit 2 stands for ▢.

Compare the numbers.

13 Which is greater, 3,819 or 3,918? ▢

14 Which is less, 7,052 or 936? ▢

15 Which is the greatest, 3,625, 4,130, or 4,031? ▢

Continue or complete each number pattern. Then state the rule.

16 6,385   6,395   ▢   6,415

Rule: ▢

17 7,821   7,521   7,221   ▢

Rule: ▢

Numbers to 100,000

Lesson Objective

- Write numbers to 100,000 in standard form, word form, and expanded form.

Learn Count on to ten thousand.

1,000 2,000 3,000 4,000 5,000 6,000 7,000 8,000 9,000 ?

	Ten Thousands	Thousands	Hundreds	Tens	Ones
9,000		●●● ●●● ●●●			

	Ten Thousands	Thousands	Hundreds	Tens	Ones
		○○○○ ○○○○ ○○			

	Ten Thousands	Thousands	Hundreds	Tens	Ones
10,000	●				

10 thousands = 1 **ten thousand**

Continued on next page

1,000 2,000 3,000 4,000 5,000 6,000 7,000 8,000 9,000 ?

Read the numbers. What number comes next?

10,000 or ten thousand

Learn **Read and show numbers in place-value charts.**

Standard form : 15,000
Word form : fifteen thousand

Ten Thousands	Thousands	Hundreds	Tens	Ones
●	●●● ●●			
1	5	0	0	0

Standard form: 73,486
Word form: seventy-three thousand, four hundred eighty-six

Ten Thousands	Thousands	Hundreds	Tens	Ones
●●● ●●● ●	●●●	●●● ●	●●● ●●● ●●	●●● ●●●
7	3	4	8	6

Guided Practice

Find the missing headings.

1 Standard form: 12,059

Word form: twelve thousand, fifty-nine

●	●●		● ● ● ● ●	● ● ● ● ● ● ● ● ●
1	2	0	5	9

Express the number in word form.

2 Standard form: 56,817

Word form:

Ten Thousands	Thousands	Hundreds	Tens	Ones
5	6	8	1	7

Express the number in standard form.

3 Word form: ten thousand, two hundred seventy-three

Ten Thousands	Thousands	Hundreds	Tens	Ones

Standard form :

Learn **Count on to one hundred thousand.**

99,996   99,997   99,998   99,999   ?

> The number that comes next is 100,000 or one hundred thousand.

10 ten thousands = 1 **hundred thousand**

Guided Practice

Express each number in word form.

4 47,048

5 90,015

6 86,300

7 70,005

Express each number in standard form.

8 ten thousand, seven hundred thirty-two

9 fifty-two thousand, one hundred

Read the number pattern. Find the number that comes next.

10 10,000   20,000   30,000   40,000   50,000

60,000   70,000   80,000   90,000

Let's Practice

Look at the place-value chart. Then express the number in word form and standard form.

Ten Thousands	Thousands	Hundreds	Tens	Ones
● ● ● ●	● ● ● ● ● ● ●		● ●	● ● ● ● ●

1 word form ▢   **2** standard form ▢

Express each number in word form.

3 43,815 ▢   **4** 90,374 ▢

5 20,505 ▢

Express each number in standard form.

6 thirty thousand, five hundred eleven ▢

7 forty-five thousand, eighty-nine ▢

ON YOUR OWN

Go to Workbook A: Practice 1, pages 1–2

 **Hands-On Activity**

WORK IN PAIRS

Materials:
- Five $10,000 bills
- Ten $1,000 bills
- Five $100 bills
- Ten $10 bills

Use the play money to show each amount. Your partner will check your answer.

1 $24,180   **2** $59,470   **3** $37,590

Learn

Find the value of each digit in a number using a place-value chart.

Look at the number 31,798.

Ten Thousands	Thousands	Hundreds	Tens	Ones
●●●	●	●●● ●●● ●	●●● ●●● ●●●	●●● ●●● ●●
3	1	7	9	8

Word form: thirty-one thousand, seven hundred ninety-eight

In 31,798,

the digit 3
- is in the ten thousands place
- stands for 3 ten thousands or 30,000
- has a value of 30,000

the digit 7
- is in the hundreds place
- stands for 7 hundreds or 700
- has a value of 700

the digit 8
- is in the ones place
- stands for 8 ones or 8
- has a value of 8.

the digit 1
- is in the thousands place
- stands for 1 thousand or 1,000
- has a value of 1,000

the digit 9
- is in the tens place
- stands for 9 tens or 90
- has a value of 90

Guided Practice

Complete.

11 In 42,653, the digit ⬚ is in the ten thousands place.

12 In 63,971, the digit 9 is in the ⬚ place.

13 In 20,974, the digit in the thousands place is ⬚.

14 In 56,301, the value of the digit 3 is ⬚.

15 In 70,569, the digit 7 stands for [   ].

16 In 82,465, the digit 2 stands for [   ].

Find the value of the digit 6 in each number.

17 **6**3,814   **18** 9**6**,781   **19** 20,5**6**3

Find the expanded form of a 5-digit number.

The **expanded form** of a number shows the value of each digit.

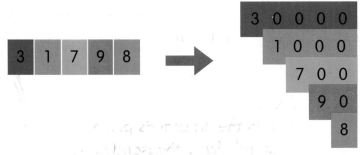

Standard form: 31,798

Word form: thirty-one thousand, seven hundred ninety-eight

Expanded form: 30,000 + 1,000 + 700 + 90 + 8

31,798 = 3 ten thousands + 1 thousand + 7 hundreds + 9 tens + 8 ones

Guided Practice

Find the missing numbers.

20 6,424 = [   ] thousands + 4 hundreds + 2 tens + 4 ones

21 18,294 = 1 ten thousand + [   ] thousands + 2 hundreds + 9 tens + 4 ones

Complete the expanded form.

22 47,093 = [   ] + 7,000 + 90 + 3

23 50,328 = [   ] + 300 + 20 + 8

24 69,417 = [   ] + [   ] + [   ] + [   ] + [   ]

WORKING TOGETHER **Game**

Find the Value!

Players: **3**
Materials:
- **10 counters**
- Blank place-value chart

STEP 1 Player 1 places the counters on the place-value chart to make a 5-digit number. Players may choose not to use all the counters.

Ten Thousands	Thousands	Hundreds	Tens	Ones
●	● ● ●	● ●		●

STEP 2 Player 2 writes the value of each digit in the 5-digit number like this:

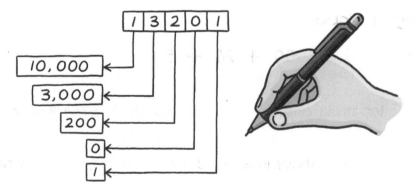

STEP 3 Player 3 checks the answer. Player 2 gets 1 point for each digit that is written correctly.

STEP 4 Switch roles and play again. Each group plays 6 rounds.

The player with the higher score wins!

Let's Practice

Complete.

1 In 20,675, the digit 0 is in the [   ] place.

2 In 76,501, the digit [   ] is in the hundreds place.

3 In 39,472, the digit [   ] is in the tens place, and the digit [   ] is in the ten thousands place.

Find the value of the digit 5 in each number.

4 27,0**5**8 [   ]

5 8**5**,027 [   ]

6 **5**2,708 [   ]

Find the missing numbers.

7 40,925 = [   ] + 900 + 20 + 5

8 32,176 = 3 ten thousands + [   ] thousands + 1 hundred + 7 tens + 6 ones

9 63,602 = [   ] ten thousands + 3 thousands + [   ] hundreds + 2 ones

10 94,057 = [   ] thousands + 5 tens + [   ] ones

ON YOUR OWN

**Go to Workbook A:
Practice 2, pages 3–6**

Lesson 1.2 Comparing Numbers to 100,000

Lesson Objectives

- Compare and order numbers to 100,000.
- Identify how much more or less one number is than another number.
- Find the rule in a number pattern.

Vocabulary

greater than (>)	greatest
less than (<)	least
more than	order

Learn **Compare 5-digit numbers using greater than and less than .**

Which number is greater, 93,085 or 76,105?

Ten Thousands	Thousands	Hundreds	Tens	Ones
9	3	0	8	5
7	6	1	0	5

Compare the number of ten thousands in the two numbers.
9 ten thousands is greater than 7 ten thousands.

So, 93,085 is greater than 76,105.
93,085 > 76,105

Which number is less, 36,520 or 37,859?

Ten Thousands	Thousands	Hundreds	Tens	Ones
3	6	5	2	0
3	7	8	5	9

First, compare the number of ten thousands in the two numbers.
They are the same.
Then, compare the number of thousands in the two numbers.
6 thousands is less than 7 thousands.

So, 36,520 is less than 37,859.
36,520 < 37,859

Guided Practice

Compare the numbers. Write > or < .

1 90,847 ⬤ 69,948

2 64,515 ⬤ 65,500

3 31,256 ⬤ 31,265

4 19,283 ⬤ 19,289

5 42,100 ⬤ 41,002

6 16,935 ⬤ 16,918

Learn **Order 5-digit numbers from greatest to least .**

Order 62,357, 9,638, and 28,986 from greatest to least.

Ten Thousands	Thousands	Hundreds	Tens	Ones
6	2	3	5	7
	9	6	3	8
2	8	9	8	6

Compare the number of ten thousands in each number.
6 ten thousands is greater than 0 ten thousands and 2 ten thousands.
62,357 is the greatest number.

2 ten thousands is greater than 0 ten thousands.
9,638 is the least number.

So, the numbers in order from greatest to least are:
62,357   28,986   9,638

Guided Practice

Order the numbers from least to greatest.

7   9,456   73,842   30,512

8   41,325   31,425   51,324   14,325

9   27,084   20,784   27,840   20,874

Learn **Compare 5-digit numbers using more than.**

Look at the numbers in the place-value chart.

Ten Thousands	Thousands	Hundreds	Tens	Ones
6	5	1	2	3
6	7	1	2	3

First, compare the number of ten thousands in the two numbers.
They are the same.
Then, compare the number of thousands in the two numbers.
65,123 is 2,000 less than 67,123.
2,000 more than 65,123 is 67,123.

Guided Practice

Look at the numbers in the place-value chart. Complete.

Ten Thousands	Thousands	Hundreds	Tens	Ones
3	7	6	2	5
	7	6	2	5

10 30,000 more than 7,625 is ⬚.

11 ⬚ is 30,000 less than 37,625.

Find the missing numbers.

12 30,000 less than 34,200 is ⬚.

13 ⬚ is 20,000 more than 53.

14 100 more than 58,967 is ⬚.

Find the rule for each number pattern. Then continue or complete the pattern.

15 2,985 2,885 ⬚ 2,685 ⬚ 2,485

16 97,642 77,642 ⬚ 37,642

17 24,701 26,702 28,703 ⬚ ⬚

18 18,079 20,079 20,279 22,279 22,479 ⬚ ⬚ 26,679

Hands-On Activity

Materials:
• Number cards

WORKING TOGETHER Work in groups of four.

STEP 1 Use four sets of number cards from 0 to 9.

STEP 2 Shuffle the number cards.
Each person takes turns drawing five number cards each.

STEP 3 Arrange your number cards to make a 5-digit number.

STEP 4 Compare your number with those made by other group members.
Then order the numbers from greatest to least.

Let's Explore!

Look at the numbers in the table.

		40,432		
		30,432		
18,432	19,432	20,432	21,432	22,432
		10,432		
		432		

1. What do you notice about the numbers across the row starting with 18,432?

2. What do you notice about the numbers down the column starting with 40,432?

3. Look at the numbers in the green boxes.
Then look at the numbers in the yellow boxes.
How are they alike?

4. Look at the numbers in the red boxes.
Then look at the numbers in the blue boxes.
How are they alike?

Let's Practice

Look at each place-value chart. Write greater than or less than.

1

Ten Thousands	Thousands	Hundreds	Tens	Ones
	8	7	6	9
2	0	1	3	1

8,769 is [   ] 20,131.

2

Ten Thousands	Thousands	Hundreds	Tens	Ones
7	0	0	2	4
5	9	9	7	8

70,024 is [   ] 59,978.

Complete the place-value chart. Order the numbers from greatest to least.

	Ten Thousands	Thousands	Hundreds	Tens	Ones
3 8,372	[ ]	[ ]	[ ]	[ ]	[ ]
4 51,030	[ ]	[ ]	[ ]	[ ]	[ ]
5 33,443	[ ]	[ ]	[ ]	[ ]	[ ]

6 From greatest to least, the numbers are [   ], [   ], and [   ].

Compare. Then complete.

72,643   79,643

7 ☐ is 7,000 less than ☐.

8 7,000 more than ☐ is ☐.

Compare. Then complete.

44,678   94,678

9 50,000 more than 44,678 is ☐.

10 ☐ is 50,000 less than 94,678.

Find the rule for each number pattern. Then continue or complete the pattern.

11 26,358   36,358   ☐   56,358   ☐
Rule: ☐

12 ☐   6,500   11,500   16,500   ☐
Rule: ☐

13 47,560   46,460   45,360   ☐   ☐
Rule: ☐

14 40,253   50,273   60,293   ☐   80,333   ☐
Rule: ☐

15 44,716   44,516   34,516   34,316   24,316   ☐   ☐
Rule: ☐

ON YOUR OWN

Go to Workbook A:
Practice 3, pages 7–12

Math Journal

Look at the numbers.

1 Explain the steps you would take to order the numbers from least to greatest.

| 4,509 | 45 | 45,009 | 450 |

2 Explain the steps you would take to order the numbers from greatest to least.
How do you know you are correct? Explain how you know.

| 2,137 | 3,721 | 2,109 | 3,748 |

Put On Your Thinking Cap!

PROBLEM SOLVING

Ten Thousands

Thousands

Hundreds

Tens

Ones

Look at the color codes above. Each color shows a place value.
Use the color codes to find the value of each puzzle.

Example

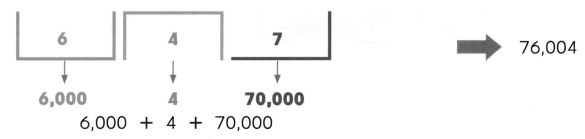

| 6 | 4 | 7 | ➡ | 76,004 |

6,000   4   70,000

6,000 + 4 + 70,000

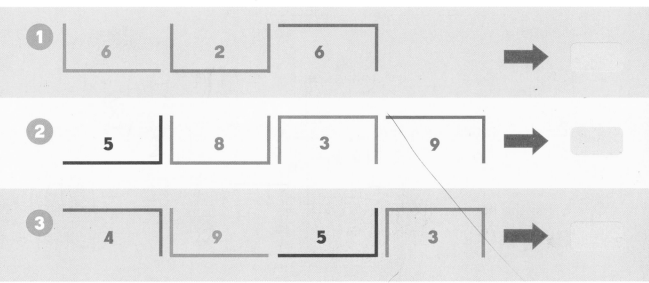

1   6   2   6   ➡

2   5   8   3   9   ➡

3   4   9   5   3   ➡

PROBLEM SOLVING

WORK IN PAIRS

4

10,000   20,000

STEP 1 Copy the number line on a sheet of paper.

STEP 2 Divide the number line into 10 equal parts and write the value of each part.

STEP 3 Write the numbers 16,500, 19,750, and 12,000 on the number line.

> First, compare the given numbers with the numbers on the number line.

5

16,500   16,600

STEP 1 Copy the number line on a sheet of paper.

STEP 2 Divide the number line into 10 equal parts and write the value of each part.

STEP 3 Write the numbers 16,560, 16,510, and 16,575 on the number line.

ON YOUR OWN

**Go to Workbook A:
Put on Your Thinking Cap!
pages 13–14**

Chapter Wrap Up

Study Guide
You have learned...

BIG IDEA

▶ Read, compare, and order numbers according to the place value of their digits.

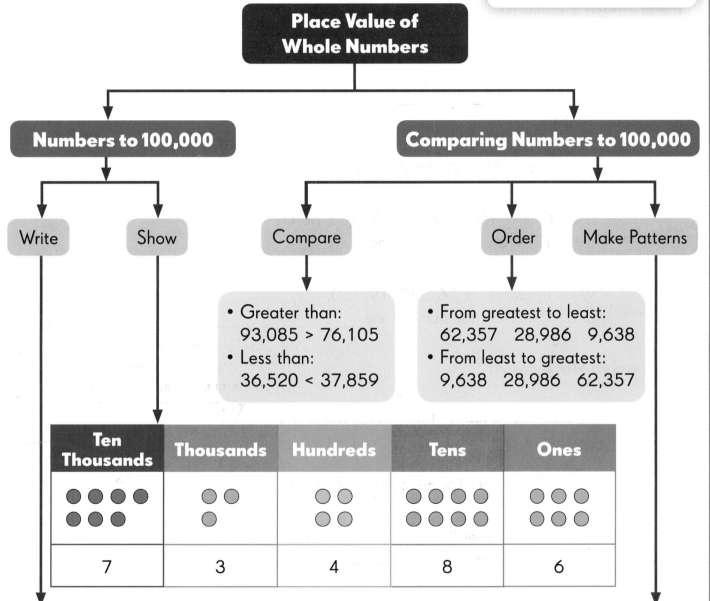

Place Value of Whole Numbers

Numbers to 100,000

Comparing Numbers to 100,000

Write

Show

Compare

Order

Make Patterns

- Greater than:
  93,085 > 76,105
- Less than:
  36,520 < 37,859

- From greatest to least:
  62,357 28,986 9,638
- From least to greatest:
  9,638 28,986 62,357

Ten Thousands	Thousands	Hundreds	Tens	Ones
7	3	4	8	6

- Standard form:
  73,486
- Word form:
  seventy-three thousand, four hundred eighty-six
- Expanded form:
  70,000 + 3,000 + 400 + 80 + 6

97,642 77,642 57,642 37,642
- 77,642 is 20,000 less than 97,642.
- 57,642 is 20,000 less than 77,642.
Rule: Subtract 20,000.

Chapter Review/Test

Vocabulary
Choose the correct word.

1 _____ , _____ , and _____ describe numbers that are compared.

2 The _____ of a number shows the place value of each digit.

3 The greatest place value in a 6-digit number is the _____ place.

> ten thousand
>
> hundred thousand
>
> place value chart
>
> greater than (>)
>
> greatest
>
> more than
>
> less than (<)
>
> least
>
> standard form
>
> expanded form
>
> word form

Concepts and Skills
Express in standard form.

4 eighty thousand, five _____

Express in word form.

5 99,215 _____

Find the value of each digit.

6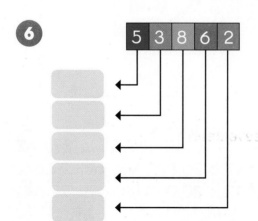

7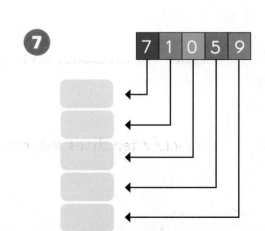

Complete.

8 In 45,876, the value of the digit 5 is ⬜ .

9 In 12,083, the digit 1 stands for ⬜ .

10 In 67,210, the digit ⬜ stands for 200.

11 In 39,813, the digit ⬜ is in the tens place.

12 In 52,981, the digit 5 is in the ⬜ place.

Complete the expanded form.

13 86,322 = ⬜ + 6,000 + 300 + ⬜ + 2

Find the mistake in the word form for each number.
Then write the correct answer.
The first one has been done for you.

Example
12,005
Word form: twelve thousand, hundred
Correct answer: twelve thousand, ~~hundred~~ five

14 76,300   seven thousand, six hundred three hundred
⬜

15 25,709   twenty-five thousand, seventy-nine
⬜

16 68,217   sixty-eight ten thousand, two hundred seventeen
⬜

Compare the numbers. Write < or >.

17 10,589 ◯ 9,875

18 56,410 ◯ 58,400

Order the numbers from least to greatest.

19 70,250 50,000 29,875

Order the numbers from greatest to least.

20 81,005 9,875 37,451

Complete.

21 10,000 greater than 56,877 is ____ .

22 2,000 less than 16,025 is ____ .

23 ____ is 40,000 less than 41,256.

**Continue or complete each number pattern.
Then state the rule.**

24 87,040 85,030 83,020

Rule:

25 5,600 10,600 10,800 15,800 16,000

Rule:

2 Estimation and Number Theory

Lessons

2.1 Estimation
2.2 Factors
2.3 Multiples

BIG IDEAS

► When two factors are multiplied, the product is a multiple of both numbers.

► Knowing factors and multiples of numbers can help in estimating products and quotients.

Recall Prior Knowledge

Using place value to find the value of each digit

Thousands	Hundreds	Tens	Ones
7	4	6	5

stands for	stands for	stands for	stands for
7 thousands or 7,000	4 hundreds or 400	6 tens or 60	5 ones or 5

In 7,465,
  the digit 7 is in the thousands place
  the digit 4 is in the hundreds place
  the digit 6 is in the tens place
  the digit 5 is in the ones place.

In 7,465,
  the digit 7 stands for 7,000
  the digit 4 stands for 400
  the digit 6 stands for 60
  the digit 5 stands for 5.

Rounding numbers to the nearest 10

Round 745 to the nearest 10.
Look at the digit to the right of the tens digit, which is the ones digit.
Round up if the ones digit is 5 or greater.
Round down if the ones digit is less than 5.

745 rounded to the nearest 10 is 750.

Rounding numbers to the nearest 100

Round 2,839 to the nearest 100.
Look at the digit to the right of the hundreds digit, which is the tens digit.
Round up if the tens digit is 5 or greater.
Round down if the tens digit is less than 5.

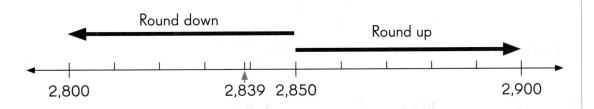

2,839 rounded to the nearest 100 is 2,800.

Estimating sums using front-end estimation

Estimate 7,615 + 2,487.
The leading digit of **7**,615 is 7.
The leading digit of **2**,487 is 2.

⑦,615 + ②,487

7,000 + 2,000 = 9,000

The estimated sum is 9,000.

Estimating differences using front-end estimation

Estimate 6,434 − 1,592.
The leading digit of **6**,434 is 6.
The leading digit of **1**,592 is 1.

⑥,434 − ①,592

6,000 − 1,000 = 5,000

The estimated difference is 5,000.

Multiplying two numbers to find the product

3 × 4 = 12

12 is the product of 3 and 4.

The product can be divided exactly by 3 and 4.

Complete.

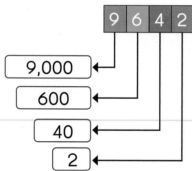

1 The digit 6 is in the [ ] place.

2 The digit 6 stands for [ ].

3 The digit 2 is in the [ ] place.

4 The digit 9 stands for [ ].

5 The digit 4 stands for [ ].

Round to the nearest 10.

6 819 is about [ ].

7 274 is about [ ].

Round to the nearest 100.

8 4,236 is about [ ].

9 5,982 is about [ ].

Estimate each sum or difference using front-end estimation.

10 Estimate 5,833 + 3,689.

$$5,833 \quad + \quad 3,689$$

$$\boxed{} \quad + \quad \boxed{} \quad = \quad \boxed{}$$

11 Estimate 5,673 − 2,568.

$$5,673 \quad - \quad 2,568$$

$$\boxed{} \quad - \quad \boxed{} \quad = \quad \boxed{}$$

Find the correct numbers.

12 $42 = 3 \times \boxed{}$

13 42 is the product of 3 and $\boxed{}$.

14 The product can be divided exactly by 3 and $\boxed{}$.

Lesson 2.1 Estimation

Lesson Objectives

- Round numbers to estimate sums, differences, products, and quotients.
- Estimate to check that an answer is reasonable.
- Decide whether an estimate or an exact answer is needed.

Vocabulary

estimate

reasonable

front-end estimation

rounding

product

quotient

Learn Use rounding to check the reasonableness of sums and differences.

Eva's Market sold 196 jars of grape jelly in September. In October, the market sold 389 jars. How many jars of grape jelly did they sell over the two months?

$$196 + 389 = 585$$

The market sold 585 jars of grape jelly altogether.

Estimate to check that the answer is **reasonable**. Round each number to the nearest hundred.

Number	Rounded to the Nearest 100
196	200
389	400

Add: $200 + 400 = 600$

The estimated sum rounded to the nearest 100 is 600.

Since both numbers are rounded up,
the estimate is greater than the actual sum.

$$196 + 389 = 585$$

$$200 + 400 = 600$$

The actual sum is close to the estimate. So, the sum is reasonable.

The answer 585 is reasonable.

The same method of estimation can be used to check the reasonableness of differences.

Guided Practice

**Find the difference. Then use rounding to check that your answer is reasonable.
Round each number to the nearest hundred.**

1 Find $786 - 453$.

$$786 - 453 = \boxed{}$$

Estimate to check that your answer is reasonable. Round each number to the nearest hundred.

Number	Rounded to the Nearest 100
786	
453	

Subtract: $\boxed{} - \boxed{} = \boxed{}$

The estimated difference rounded to the nearest 100 is $\boxed{}$.

Is your answer reasonable?

Explain: $\boxed{}$

Learn Use **front-end estimation** to check the reasonableness of sums and differences.

Find 7,840 − 3,622.

7,840 − 3,622 = 4,218

The answer is 4,218.

Estimate to check that the answer is reasonable.

⑦,840 − ③,622

7,000 − 3,000 = 4,000

The estimated difference is 4,000.

4,218 is close to 4,000. So, the answer is reasonable.

The answer 4,218 is reasonable.

The same method of estimation can be used to check the reasonableness of sums.

Guided Practice

Find the sum. Then use front-end estimation to check that your answer is reasonable.

2 Find 6,572 + 8,144.

6,572 + 8,144 = ⬚

The answer is ⬚ .

Estimate to check that your answer is reasonable.

6,572 + 8,144

⬚ + ⬚ = ⬚

The estimated sum is ⬚ .

Is your answer reasonable?

Explain: ⬚

Find each sum or difference. Then use rounding or front-end estimation to check that your answers are reasonable. Round each number to the nearest hundred.

3 $5{,}426 + 3{,}210 = $

4 $8{,}475 - 3{,}356 = $

5 $9{,}633 + 4{,}250 = $

6 $16{,}862 - 12{,}551 = $

Learn **Use rounding to check the reasonableness of products.**

Santos bought 2 cartons of single cup coffee pods, each containing 326 coffee pods.
Find the total number of coffee pods in the cartons.

$326 \times 2 = 652$

The total number of coffee pods is 652.

Estimate to check that the answer is reasonable.

Round 326 to the nearest hundred and multiply by 2.

Number	Rounded to the Nearest 100 × 2
326	$300 \times 2 = 600$

The estimated product rounded to the nearest 100 is 600.

The answer 652 is reasonable.

Since 326 is rounded down, the estimate
is less than the actual product.

$$326 \times 2 = 652$$
$$\downarrow \qquad \qquad \downarrow$$
$$300 \times 2 = 600$$

652 is close to 600, so the answer is reasonable.

Guided Practice

Find the product. Then use rounding to check that your answer is reasonable. Round the 3-digit number to the nearest hundred.

7 Find 242 × 4.

242 × 4 = [ ]

The answer is [ ] .

Estimate to check that your answer is reasonable.

Round 242 to the nearest hundred and multiply by 4.

Number	Rounded to the Nearest 100 × 4
242	[ ] × 4 = [ ]

The estimated product rounded to the nearest 100 is [ ] .

Is your answer reasonable?

Explain: [ ]

Use front-end estimation to check the reasonableness of products.

Find 134 × 5.

134 × 5 = 670

The answer is 670.

Estimate to check that the answer is reasonable.
Multiply the value of the digits in the greatest place of each number.

①34 × 5
↓
100 × 5 = 500

1 hundred × 5 = 5 hundreds or 500

The estimated product is 500.

The answer 670 is reasonable.

670 is close to 500. So, the answer is reasonable.

Guided Practice

Find the product. Then use front-end estimation to check that your answer is reasonable.

8 Find 471 × 2.

471 × 2 = [ ]

The answer is [ ].

Estimate to check that your answer is reasonable.

④71 × 2

[ ] × 2 = [ ]

The estimated product is [ ].

Is your answer reasonable?

Explain: [ ]

Learn **Use related multiplication facts to check the reasonableness of quotients .**

Novak bought a box of 72 building blocks. He shared the blocks equally with his 2 friends. How many blocks did each of them get?

72 ÷ 3 = 24

Each of them got 24 blocks.

Use related multiplication facts to check that your answer is reasonable. Since division is the opposite of multiplication, find a multiple of 3 that is close to 7.

3 × 2 = 6   3 × 20 = 60

3 × 3 = 9   3 × 30 = 90

72 is closer to 60 than to 90.

So, 72 ÷ 3 is about 60 ÷ 3.

60 ÷ 3 = 20

The estimated quotient is 20.
The answer 24 is reasonable.

24 is close to 20. So, the answer is reasonable.

Guided Practice

Find each quotient. Then use related multiplication facts to check that your answers are reasonable.

9 Find $92 \div 2$.

$92 \div 2 = $ [____]

The answer is [____].

Use related multiplication facts to check that your answer is reasonable. Since division is the opposite of multiplication, find a multiple of 2 that is close to 9.

$2 \times 40 = $ [____] $2 \times 50 = $ [____]

92 is closer to [____] than to [____].

So, $92 \div 2$ is about [____] $\div 2$.

[____] $\div 2 = $ [____]

The estimated quotient is [____].

Is your answer reasonable?

Explain: [____]

10 Find $76 \div 4$.

$76 \div 4 = $ [____]

The answer is [____].

Use related multiplication facts to check that your answer is reasonable. Since division is the opposite of multiplication, find a multiple of 4 that is close to 7.

$4 \times $ [____] $= $ [____] $4 \times $ [____] $= $ [____]

76 is closer to [____] than to [____].

So, $76 \div 4$ is about [____] $\div 4$.

[____] $\div 4 = $ [____]

The estimated quotient is [____].

Is your answer reasonable?

Explain: [____]

11 Find 85 ÷ 5.

85 ÷ 5 = [ ]

The answer is [ ] .

Use related multiplication facts to check that your answer is reasonable.
Since division is the opposite of multiplication, find a multiple of 5 that is close to 8.

5 × [ ] = [ ]

5 × [ ] = [ ]

85 is closer to [ ] than to [ ] .

So, 85 ÷ 5 is about [ ] ÷ 5.

[ ] ÷ 5 = [ ]

The estimated quotient is [ ] .

Is your answer reasonable?

Explain: [ ]

Find each product or quotient. Then use one of the methods above to check that your answers are reasonable.

12 123 × 7 = [ ]

Estimate: [ ]

Is your answer reasonable?

Explain: [ ]

13 54 ÷ 3 = [ ]

Estimate: [ ]

Is your answer reasonable?

Explain: [ ]

14 323 × 3 = [ ]

Estimate: [ ]

Is your answer reasonable?

Explain: [ ]

15 96 ÷ 4 = [ ]

Estimate: [ ]

Is your answer reasonable?

Explain: [ ]

Let's Explore!

Use two methods to estimate.

Example

Estimate 73 ÷ 8.

Method 1

73 is close to 72.
So, 73 ÷ 8 ⟶ 72 ÷ 8 = 9.

Method 2

8 × 8 = 64
8 × 9 = 72
8 × 10 = 80
8 × 9 = 72 is the closest to 73, so the estimated quotient is 9.

Example

Estimate 9 × 26.

Method 1

9 is close to 10.
So, 9 × 26 ⟶ 10 × 26 = 260.

Method 2

9 × 26 ⟶ 9 × 25 = 225

Method 3

9 × 26 ⟶ 10 × 25 = 250

1 658 ÷ 8

2 6 × 52

Learn **Decide whether to find an estimate or an exact answer.**

The Senior Citizen Committee has raised $1,000
for the Senior Center.
Is $1,000 enough to buy the items shown?
Decide if you need an exact answer or an estimate.

$599
Television set

$705
Used piano

Estimate the total cost by rounding to the nearest hundred dollars.
$600 + $700 = $1,300
The committee does not have enough money to buy both items.

An estimate is all that is needed to decide if the committee
has enough money to buy both items.

About how much more money does the committee need
to buy both items?

Because the question asks **about** how much more money
is needed, an estimate is needed.

$1,300 − $1,000 = $300
The committee needs about $300 more to buy both items.

. . . .

4 people are invited to Marcia's home. Each guest gets one carton
of cranberry juice, which costs 45¢. How much money does Marcia need to buy
the juice?

Because the question asks **how much** money Marcia needs to buy
the juice, an exact answer is needed.

4 × 45 = 180 cents = $1.80

She needs $1.80 to buy the juice.

Guided Practice

Solve. Decide whether to find an estimate or an exact answer.

16 The table shows the number of dogs that were adopted in a state within a year.

Dogs Adopted in a Year	Number
Mixed-breed adults	12,760
Pure-bred adults	17,432
Puppies	20,979

How many dogs were adopted altogether that year?

17 Mr. Sousa has $250. He wants to spend $63 on a sweatshirt, $45 on running shoes, and $120 on sports gear.
Does he have enough money?

18 A family has 7 people. Each person is supposed to drink $\frac{7}{8}$ quart of water every day. About how much water is needed for the whole family each day?

19 Kerry bought 15 roasted chickens. Each chicken cost $6.
Find the total amount Kerry spent on the chickens.

20 Joel bought 3 apples at 26 cents each and 4 oranges at 32 cents each. About how much money did he spend on the apples and oranges?

Let's Practice

Find each sum or difference. Then use rounding or front-end estimation to check that your answers are reasonable. Round each number to the nearest hundred.

1 $536 + 289 + 109 =$

2 $320 + 478 + 215 =$

3 $8,530 - 1,286 =$

4 $7,271 + 1,335 =$

5 $26,235 - 1,451 =$

6 $15,422 + 13,130 =$

7 $18,726 + 29,343 =$

8 $31,540 - 24,622 =$

Find each product. Then use rounding or front-end estimation to check your answers. Round the 3-digit number to the nearest hundred.

9 $232 \times 4 =$

10 $148 \times 5 =$

11 $212 \times 3 =$

12 $498 \times 2 =$

Find each quotient. Then use related multiplication facts to check your answers.

13 $42 \div 3 =$

14 $56 \div 2 =$

15 $80 \div 5 =$

16 $88 \div 4 =$

Solve. Decide whether to find an estimate or an exact answer.

17 A rectangular lawn is 11 meters long and 4 meters wide. About how many square meters of grass sod is needed to cover the entire lawn?

18 A rectangular courtyard is 12 feet long and 8 feet wide. A tile is 2 feet long and 2 feet wide. How many tiles are needed to pave the courtyard?

ON YOUR OWN

Go to Workbook A:
Practice 1, pages 15–20

Lesson 2.2 Factors

Lesson Objectives

- Find the common factors and greatest common factor of two whole numbers.
- Identify prime numbers and composite numbers.

Vocabulary

factor

common factor

greatest common factor

prime number

composite number

Learn Break down whole numbers into factors.

$$1 \times 6 = 6$$

Can 6 be divided exactly by 1?
Yes. So, 1 is a factor of 6.

Can 6 be divided exactly by 6?
Yes. So, 6 is a factor of 6.

6 is the product of 1 and 6.
1 and 6 are **factors** of 6.

When a number can be divided exactly by another number, there is no remainder.

$$2 \times 3 = 6 \qquad\qquad 3 \times 2 = 6$$

Can 6 be divided exactly by 2? Yes. So 2 is a factor of 6.
Can 6 be divided exactly by 3? Yes. So 3 is also a factor of 6.
Can 6 be divided exactly by 4? No. So 4 is not a factor of 6.
Can 6 be divided exactly by 5? No. So 5 is not a factor of 6.

6 is a product of 2 and 3.
2 and 3 are factors of 6.

The factors of 6 are 1, 2, 3, and 6.

Guided Practice

Find the factors of 32.

1. $32 = 1 \times 32$

   $32 = 2 \times 16$

   $32 = 4 \times 8$

   The factors of 32 are ⬚ , ⬚ , ⬚ , ⬚ , ⬚ , and ⬚ .

Find the factors of 24.

2. $24 = $ ⬚ $\times$ ⬚

3. $24 = $ ⬚ $\times$ ⬚

4. $24 = $ ⬚ $\times$ ⬚

5. $24 = $ ⬚ $\times$ ⬚

6. The factors of 24 are ⬚ , ⬚ , ⬚ , ⬚ , ⬚ , ⬚ , ⬚ , and ⬚ .

^{Learn} Determine if one number is a factor of another.

Is 3 a factor of 12?

Divide 12 by 3.

```
      4
3) 1 2
   1 2
   ───
     0
```

12 can be divided exactly by 3.
So, 3 is a factor of 12.

Is 5 a factor of 16?

Divide 16 by 5.

```
      3
5) 1 6
   1 5
   ───
     1
```

16 cannot be divided exactly by 5.
So, 5 is not a factor of 16.

Guided Practice

Find the factors of each number.

7 12

8 28

9 56

10 100

^{Learn} Find common factors of two whole numbers.

What are the common factors of 8 and 12?

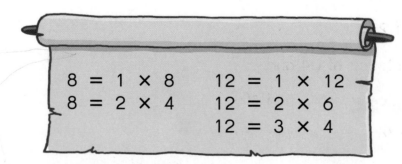

```
8 = 1 × 8        12 = 1 × 12
8 = 2 × 4        12 = 2 × 6
                 12 = 3 × 4
```

The factors of 8 are (1), (2), (4), and 8.

The factors of 12 are (1), (2), 3, (4), 6, and 12.

The **common factors** of 8 and 12 are 1, 2, and 4.

A common factor is shared by two or more numbers.

Guided Practice

Find the common factors of 9 and 36.

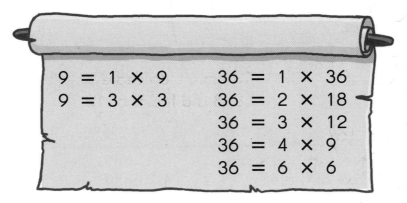

9 = 1 × 9   36 = 1 × 36
9 = 3 × 3   36 = 2 × 18
                 36 = 3 × 12
                 36 = 4 × 9
                 36 = 6 × 6

11 The factors of 9 are [ ] , [ ] , and [ ] .

12 The factors of 36 are [ ] , [ ] , [ ] , [ ] , [ ] , [ ] , [ ] , [ ] , and [ ] .

13 The common factors of 9 and 36 are [ ] , [ ] , and [ ] .

Complete. Write yes or no.

14 Is 5 a factor of 20? [ ]

15 Is 5 a factor of 35? [ ]

16 Is 5 a common factor of 20 and 35? [ ]

17 Is 2 a factor of 24? [ ]

18 Is 2 a factor of 27? [ ]

19 Is 2 a common factor of 24 and 27? [ ]

20 Is 3 a common factor of 30 and 40? [ ]

21 Is 4 a common factor of 96 and 48? [ ]

Find the common factors of each pair of numbers.

22 32 and 12 [ ]   **23** 12 and 16 [ ]

24 60 and 54 [ ]   **25** 45 and 96 [ ]

^Learn **Find the** greatest common factor **of two whole numbers.**

Find the greatest common factor of 8 and 12.

Method 1

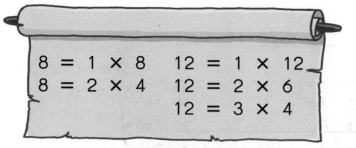

8 = 1 × 8	12 = 1 × 12
8 = 2 × 4	12 = 2 × 6
	12 = 3 × 4

Step 1 The factors of 8 are (1), (2), (4), and 8.

The factors of 12 are (1), (2), 3, (4), 6, and 12.

The common factors of 8 and 12 are 1, 2, and 4.

Step 2 Compare the common factors.
The greatest common factor of 8 and 12 is 4.

1, 2, and 4 are common factors of 8 and 12.

Method 2

You can find the greatest common factor by division.

Step 1 Divide 8 and 12 by a common factor.

```
2 | 8,      12
    4,       6
    ↑        ↑
  8 ÷ 2   12 ÷ 2
```

Step 2 Divide until the numbers cannot be divided by a common factor other than 1.

```
2 | 8,      12
2 | 4,       6
    2,       3
    ↑        ↑
  4 ÷ 2    6 ÷ 2
```

2 and 3 have no common factor other than 1.

Step 3 Multiply the common factors.

```
2 × 2 = 4  ←  (2)| 8,      12
              (2)| 4,       6
                   2,       3
```

4 is the greatest common factor.

Guided Practice

Find the greatest common factor of 16 and 48.

Method 1

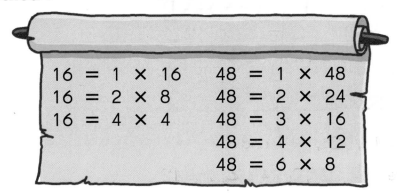

16 = 1 × 16   48 = 1 × 48
16 = 2 × 8   48 = 2 × 24
16 = 4 × 4   48 = 3 × 16
               48 = 4 × 12
               48 = 6 × 8

26 The factors of 16 are ⬚ , ⬚ , ⬚ , ⬚ , and ⬚ .

27 The factors of 48 are ⬚ , ⬚ , ⬚ , ⬚ , ⬚ , ⬚ , ⬚ , ⬚ , ⬚ , and ⬚ .

28 The common factors of 16 and 48 are ⬚ , ⬚ , ⬚ , ⬚ , and ⬚ .

29 The greatest common factor of 16 and 48 is ⬚ .

Method 2

30 8 | 16,   48
        ⬚ ⬚ , ⬚

        ⬚ , ⬚

    8 × ⬚ = ⬚

    The greatest common factor of 16 and 48 is ⬚ .

Find the greatest common factor.

31 Find the greatest common factor of 18 and 72. ⬚

Identify prime numbers and composite numbers.

Find all the factors of 5.

$$5 = 1 \times 5$$

The factors of 5 are 1 and 5.

> A prime number has only 2 different factors, 1 and the number itself.
> 5 is a prime number.

Find all the factors of 12.

$$12 = 1 \times 12$$
$$12 = 2 \times 6$$
$$12 = 3 \times 4$$

The factors of 12 are 1, 2, 3, 4, 6, and 12.

> A composite number has more than 2 different factors.
> 12 has 6 factors, so it is a composite number.

Find all the factors of 1.

$$1 \times 1 = 1$$
The number 1 has only 1 factor. | 1 is neither prime nor composite.

Guided Practice

Find all the factors. Then decide whether the numbers are prime or composite.

32 21

33 33

34 59

35 77

 **Hands-On Activity**

1 How do you find the prime numbers from 1 to 20?

STEP 1 2 is the first prime number. It is underlined.
Cross out 1 since it is neither a prime nor a composite number.
Cross out all the greater numbers that can be divided exactly by 2.
The first of these numbers has been crossed out for you.

X	2	3	X	5	6	7	8	9	10
11	12	13	14	15	16	17	18	19	20

STEP 2 Ask your partner to find the first number after 2 that has not been crossed out and underline it. It is the next prime number.
Then cross out all the greater numbers that can be divided exactly by 3.

STEP 3 Continue taking turns underlining the next prime number and crossing out the numbers that can be divided exactly by it.
Which numbers are underlined?
These are the prime numbers between 1 and 20.

2 Use the same method to find all the prime numbers from 1 to 50.

1	2	3	4	5	6	7	8	9	10
11	12	13	14	15	16	17	18	19	20
21	22	23	24	25	26	27	28	29	30
31	32	33	34	35	36	37	38	39	40
41	42	43	44	45	46	47	48	49	50

Let's Explore!

WORK IN PAIRS

Use these numbers to complete the activity.

2, 5, 6, 8, 9, 11, 14, 15, 18, 20, 22,
23, 25, 30, 32, 43, 37, 38, 40, 45

1 Divide each number by 2. Then complete the table.

Numbers that can be Divided Exactly by 2	Numbers that cannot be Divided Exactly by 2

a What do you notice about all the numbers in the box on the left?

b What can you say about all the numbers in the box on the right?

2 Divide each number by 5. Then complete the table.

Numbers that can be Divided Exactly by 5	Numbers that cannot be Divided Exactly by 5

a What do you notice about all the numbers in the box on the left?

b What can you say about all the numbers in the box on the right?

Let's Practice

Think about multiplication and division. Then find the missing numbers.

1 28 = 1 × [ ]

28 ÷ 1 = [ ]

2 28 = 2 × [ ]

28 ÷ 2 = [ ]

3 28 = 4 × [ ]

28 ÷ 4 = [ ]

4 The factors of 28 are [ ], [ ], [ ], [ ], [ ], and [ ].

Find all the factors of 42.

5 42 = [ ] × [ ]

6 42 = [ ] × [ ]

7 42 = [ ] × [ ]

8 42 = [ ] × [ ]

9 The factors of 42 are [ ], [ ], [ ], [ ], [ ], [ ], [ ], and [ ].

Complete.

10 The factors of 8 are [ ], [ ], [ ], and [ ].

11 The factors of 24 are [ ], [ ], [ ], [ ], [ ], [ ], [ ], and [ ].

12 The common factors of 8 and 24 are [ ], [ ], [ ], and [ ].

13 The greatest common factor of 8 and 24 is [ ].

14 The factors of 52 are [ ], [ ], [ ], [ ], [ ], and [ ].

15 The common factors of 24 and 52 are [ ], [ ], and [ ].

16 The greatest common factor of 24 and 52 is [ ].

Answer each question.

6, 14, 15, 20, 23, 25, 28, 32, 33, 35, 39

17 Which of these numbers have 2 as a factor? ⬜

18 Which of these numbers have 5 as a factor? ⬜

Find a possible number which has only these factors.

Factors of a Number

Factors	Number
19 1, 2, 3, and 6	
20 1, 2, 5, and 10	

Complete.

21 Find all the prime numbers from 1 to 10. ⬜

22 Find all the prime numbers for each set of numbers. Complete the table.

Prime Numbers

1 to 16	16 to 32	32 to 48

Which set has more prime numbers? ⬜

Solve.

23 Julia's birthday is on 3/7/1998. Using the digits from her birthday, form three 2-digit prime numbers, and three 2-digit composite numbers.

ON YOUR OWN

Go to Workbook A:
Practice 2, pages 21–26

READING AND WRITING MATH
Math Journal

Example

These are the steps to find the factors of 12.

STEP 1 Think of all the numbers that divide 12 exactly.

12 ÷ 1 = 12	12 ÷ 4 = 3
12 ÷ 2 = 6	12 ÷ 6 = 2
12 ÷ 3 = 4	12 ÷ 12 = 1

Think of the
multiplication tables.
$$12 = 1 \times 12$$
$$12 = 2 \times 6$$
$$12 = 3 \times 4$$

STEP 2 The factors are 1, 2, 3, 4, 6, and 12.

Write the steps for finding the common factors of 12 and 15.

Lesson 2.3 Multiples

Lesson Objectives

- Find multiples of whole numbers.
- Find common multiples and the least common multiple of 2 or more numbers.

Vocabulary

multiple

common multiple

least common multiple

Learn Find multiples of a number.

To find a multiple of a number, multiply that number by any whole number.

What are the multiples of 3?

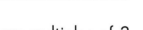

Say the multiplication table of 3.

$1 \times 3 = 3$	$2 \times 3 = 6$	$3 \times 3 = 9$
$4 \times 3 = 12$	$5 \times 3 = 15$	$6 \times 3 = 18$
$7 \times 3 = 21$	$8 \times 3 = 24$	$9 \times 3 = 27$
$10 \times 3 = 30$		

3, 6, 9, 12, 15, 18, 21, 24, 27, and 30 are multiples of 3.

Learn Determine whether a number is a multiple of another number.

Is 12 a multiple of 3?

```
      4
  3)1 2
    1 2
    ───
      0
```

12 can be divided exactly by 3.
So, 12 is a multiple of 3.
3 is a factor of 12.

Is 28 a multiple of 3?

```
      9
  3)2 8
    2 7
    ───
      1
```

28 cannot be divided exactly by 3.
So, 28 is not a multiple of 3.
3 is not a factor of 28.

3 is a factor of all the multiples of 3.

Guided Practice

Complete. Write yes or no.

1 Is 24 a multiple of 8? ____

2 Is 42 a multiple of 5? ____

Find the first twelve multiples of a number.

What are the first twelve multiples of 7?

1 × 7 = **7**	2 × 7 = **14**	3 × 7 = **21**
4 × 7 = **28**	5 × 7 = **35**	6 × 7 = **42**
7 × 7 = **49**	8 × 7 = **56**	9 × 7 = **63**
10 × 7 = **70**	11 × 7 = **77**	12 × 7 = **84**

7, 14, 21, 28 ... 84 are the first twelve multiples of 7.

The first multiple of 7 is 7.

The second multiple of 7 is 14.

The third multiple of 7 is 21.

> 7 is a factor of all the multiples of 7.
> 7 is a factor of 7.
> 7 is a factor of 14.
> 7 is a factor of 21.

Guided Practice

Find the first five multiples of each number.

3 2 ____

4 10 ____

5 6 ____

6 8 ____

Complete.

7 What is the fourth multiple of 7? ____

8 What is the fifth multiple of 7? ____

9 What is the twelfth multiple of 7? ____

Learn **Find common multiples of two whole numbers.**

What is a common multiple of 3 and 5?

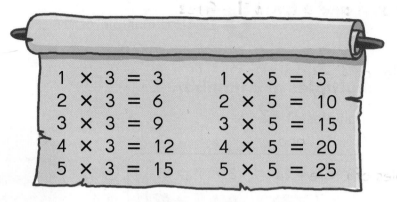

$$1 \times 3 = 3 \qquad 1 \times 5 = 5$$
$$2 \times 3 = 6 \qquad 2 \times 5 = 10$$
$$3 \times 3 = 9 \qquad 3 \times 5 = 15$$
$$4 \times 3 = 12 \qquad 4 \times 5 = 20$$
$$5 \times 3 = 15 \qquad 5 \times 5 = 25$$

The multiples of 3 are 3, 6, 9, 12, (15) ...

The multiples of 5 are 5, 10, (15), 20, 25 ...

> A number that is a multiple of two or more numbers is a common multiple. A common multiple of 3 and 5 is 15.

What are the common multiples of 3 and 4?

The multiples of 3 are 3, 6, 9, (12), 15, 18, 21, (24), 27, 30, 33, (36) ...

The multiples of 4 are 4, 8, (12), 16, 20, (24), 28, 32, (36), 40 ...

3 and 4 have more than one common multiple.

Three of their common multiples are 12, 24, and 36.

Compare the common multiples.

> A common multiple that is less than all the others is called the **least common multiple**. 12 is the least common multiple of 3 and 4.

You will find more common multiples if you continue.

Guided Practice

List the first twelve multiples of 4 and 6. Then find the common multiples of 4 and 6 from the first twelve multiples.

10 The first twelve multiples of 4 are ▢ , ▢ , ▢ , ▢ , ▢ ,

▢ , ▢ , ▢ , ▢ , ▢ ,

and ▢ .

11 The first twelve multiples of 6 are ▢ , ▢ , ▢ , ▢ , ▢ ,

▢ , ▢ , ▢ , ▢ , ▢ ,

and ▢ .

12 From the list of twelve multiples, the common multiples of 4 and 6 are

▢ , ▢ , ▢ , and ▢ .

13 The least common multiple of 4 and 6 is ▢ .

Complete.

14 List the first twelve multiples of 5 and 8. From the list, find
a common multiple of 5 and 8. ▢

Find a common multiple of each pair of numbers.

15 3 and 4 ▢   **16** 5 and 4 ▢   **17** 2 and 7 ▢

Solve.

18 15 and 30 are common multiples of 5 and X. X is a 1-digit number.
X is not 1. What number is X? ▢

19 Make a list of the multiples of 3 and 7. Find the first three common multiples
of 3 and 7. Which is the least common multiple? ▢

Learn **Find the least common multiple of two whole numbers.**

Find the least common multiple of 30 and 48.

$$
\begin{array}{r|rr}
2 & 30, & 48 \\
\hline
3 & 15, & 24 \\
\hline
& 5, & 8
\end{array}
$$

Divide 30 and 48 until they cannot be divided by a common factor other than 1.

5 and 8 have no common factor other than 1.

Multiply the four factors.

$2 \times 3 \times 5 \times 8 = 240$

So, 240 is the least common multiple of 30 and 48.

Guided Practice

Find the least common multiple of each pair of numbers using the division method.

20 12 and 26

$$
\begin{array}{r|rr}
2 & 12, & 26 \\
\hline
& \boxed{}, & \boxed{}
\end{array}
$$

The least common multiple of 12 and 26 is $\boxed{}$.

21 15 and 21

$$
\begin{array}{r|rr}
\boxed{} & 15, & 21 \\
\hline
& \boxed{}, & \boxed{}
\end{array}
$$

The least common multiple of 15 and 21 is $\boxed{}$.

Let's Practice

Find the first five multiples of each number.

1 9

2 7

Find the numbers in the box that are multiples of each given number.

| 6 | 16 | 18 | 27 | 36 | 42 | 63 |

3 4

4 9

Complete.

5 List the first twelve multiples of 6 and 8. From the list, find the common multiples of 6 and 8.

Solve.

Here is a list of numbers. Circle the multiples of 5. Two of the multiples of 5 are common multiples of 5 and X.

| 4 | 5 | 7 | 10 | 15 | 24 | 25 | 27 | 35 | 42 | 45 | 49 |

6 What number is X?

7 From the list, what are the common multiples of 5 and X?

Find the least common multiple of each pair of numbers.

8 4 and 9

9 5 and 8

10 12 and 56

Solve.

11 12 is the least common multiple of 4 and X.
Find three possible values of X.

ON YOUR OWN

**Go to Workbook A:
Practice 3, pages 27–30**

PROBLEM SOLVING

1   Mrs. Lim wrote a number on a card without showing
    it to her students.
    She asked her students what the number was.
    She gave them only three hints.
    •   The number can be divided exactly by 3.
    •   When I add 3 to the number, it can be divided exactly by 5.
    •   The number is less than 32 but greater than 23.
    What is the number?

First make a list of the
multiples of 3 and the
multiples of 5.

2   Jonathan bought an item that cost less than $100. He could pay
    for the item exactly with only $20 bills. He could also pay for the
    item exactly with only $5 bills. What were the likely prices of the
    item he bought?

Put On Your Thinking Cap!

PROBLEM SOLVING

3 A farmer has a rectangular field. The length of the field is 5 times its width. The length and width are whole numbers. The perimeter of the field is 50 meters when rounded to the nearest ten meters. What are the width and length of the field?

On a sheet of paper, record your answers in a table like this:

Width	Length	Perimeter	Perimeter Rounded to the Nearest 10 m
1st guess: 1 m	5 m	1 + 1 + 5 + 5 = 12 m	10 m
2nd guess:			

ON YOUR OWN

Go to Workbook A: Put on Your Thinking Cap! pages 31–34

Chapter Wrap Up

Study Guide
You have learned...

	Estimation
	To estimate

To estimate
- the sum of two or three numbers using rounding or front-end estimation
- the difference of two numbers using rounding or front-end estimation
- the product of a 3-digit number and a 1-digit number using rounding or front-end estimation of the 3-digit number
- the quotient when a 3-digit number is divided by a 1-digit number using related multiplication facts.

To decide whether to estimate or find an exact answer.

Round to the Nearest Hundred	Front-end Estimation
147 + 781 = 928 ⟶ 100 + 800 = 900	147 + 781 ↓ 100 + 700 = 800
8,412 − 1,951 = 6,461 ⟶ 8,400 − 2,000 = 6,400	8,412 − 1,951 ↓ 8,000 − 1,000 = 7,000
267 × 7 = 1,869 ⟶ 300 × 7 = 2,100	267 × 7 = 1,869 200 × 7 = 1,400

Estimate Quotients using Related Multiplication Facts

- To estimate 546 ÷ 6,
  6 × 90 = 540   6 × 100 = 600
  546 is closer to 540 than to 600. 540 ÷ 6 = 90
  The estimated quotient is 90.

Number Theory

Factors and Multiples

- To find the factors and common factors of numbers.
- To identify prime and composite numbers.
- To find the multiples and common multiples of numbers.

Number	Factors	Common Factors	Greatest Common Factor
8	1, 2, 4, and 8	1, 2, and 4	4
12	1, 2, 3, 4, 6, and 12		

Number	Factors	Prime or Composite?
7	1 and 7	Prime, because the only factors are 1 and the number itself.
8	1, 2, 4, and 8	Composite, because there are more than 2 factors.

Number	Multiples	Common Multiples	Least Common Multiple
3	3, 6, 9, 12, 15, 18, 21, 24, 27, 30, 33, 36 …	12, 24, and 36	12
4	4, 8, 12, 16, 20, 24, 28, 32, 36 …		

Chapter Review/Test

Vocabulary

Choose the correct word.

estimate
factor
rounding
reasonable
front-end estimation
composite number
prime number
greatest common factor
least common multiple
product
quotient
multiple

1 You can _____ to check that an answer is reasonable.

2 A number that has only 2 different factors is a _____ .

3 6 is a _____ of 36, and 36 is a _____ of 6.

4 The _____ of two or more numbers is less than all other common multiples.

5 When one number is multiplied by another, the result is called a _____ .

Concepts and Skills

Find each sum or difference. Then use rounding to check that your answers are reasonable. Round each number to its greatest place value.

6 $74 + 53 = $ _____

7 $216 - 39 = $ _____

8 $568 + 329 = $ _____

9 $707 - 183 = $ _____

Find each sum or difference. Then use front-end estimation to check that your answers are reasonable.

10 $23 + 64 = $ _____

11 $31 - 19 = $ _____

12 $516 + 724 = $ _____

13 $926 - 654 = $ _____

14 $8,142 + 3,154 = $ _____

15 $7,214 - 3,645 = $ _____

Find each product or quotient. Then estimate to check that your answers are reasonable.

(16) 42 × 3 = ⬚

(17) 231 × 4 = ⬚

(18) 93 ÷ 3 = ⬚

(19) 70 ÷ 5 = ⬚

Complete. Then estimate to check that your answers are reasonable.

(20) 8,012 + 1,569 = ⬚

(21) 568 − 127 = ⬚

(22) 3,516 − 1,657 = ⬚

(23) 59 × 6 = ⬚

(24) 72 ÷ 3 = ⬚

(25) 78 × 5 = ⬚

(26) 84 ÷ 2 = ⬚

(27) 44 × 8 = ⬚

(28) 56 ÷ 4 = ⬚

(29) 96 ÷ 3 = ⬚

(30) 109 × 7 = ⬚

(31) 95 ÷ 5 = ⬚

Find the factors of each number.

(32) 16 ⬚

(33) 36 ⬚

Complete.

(34) Find the common factors of 16 and 36 ⬚ .

(35) The greatest common factor of 16 and 36 is ⬚ .

Find the first eight multiples of each number.

(36) 4 ⬚

(37) 5 ⬚

Complete.

38 Find a common multiple of 4 and 5.

39 The least common multiple of 4 and 5 is [ ].

Find the factors of each number. Then list the prime numbers and composite numbers.

| 23 | 32 | 9 | 1,851 | 37 | 79 |

40 Prime numbers [ ]

Composite numbers [ ]

Problem Solving

Solve. Decide whether to find the estimate or the exact answer.

41 Jared has 98 oranges. He packs them into 4 crates. How many oranges does he have left over?

42 There are 147 erasers, 215 pencils, and 327 pens in a stationery shop. About how many erasers, pencils, and pens are there altogether?

43 A tourist agency is expecting 83 visitors in a week. Each of the agency's cars can carry 4 passengers. How many cars will be needed for all the visitors?

44 Ms. Clarkson has $315 to spend on kitchen appliances. She has to choose between two of three options; a microwave for $220, a coffee machine for $83, and a waffle maker for $98. Should she buy the microwave and the coffee machine, or the microwave and the waffle maker?

Chapter 3
Whole Number Multiplication and Division

Lessons

3.1 Multiplying by a 1-Digit Number

3.2 Multiplying by a 2-Digit Number

3.3 Modeling Division with Regrouping

3.4 Dividing by a 1-Digit Number

3.5 Real-World Problems: Multiplication and Division

BIG IDEAS

▶ Place value is used to multiply and divide multi-digit numbers.

▶ Estimation can be used to check the reasonableness of an answer.

Recall Prior Knowledge

Multiplication is like repeated addition

Find 5×3.
Recall how many are there in 5 groups of 3.

$$5 \times 3 = 5 \text{ groups of } 3$$
$$= 3 + 3 + 3 + 3 + 3$$
$$= 15$$

Division is like repeated subtraction

Find $12 \div 4$.
Recall how many groups of 4 are in 12.

$12 - 4 = 8$ means taking away a group of 4 to leave 8.
$8 - 4 = 4$ means taking away another group of 4 to leave 4.
$4 - 4 = 0$ means taking away another group of 4 to leave 0.
There are 3 groups of 4 in 12.

So, $12 \div 4 = 3$.

Multiplying mentally by skip counting or recalling multiplication facts

Find 7×6 by skip counting.

So, $7 \times 6 = 42$.

> I skip count in 6s.
> 6, 12, 18, 24, 30, 36, 42

Find 400×8 using related multiplication facts.

$$4 \times 8 = 32$$
$$40 \times 8 = 320$$
$$400 \times 8 = 3,200$$

Multiplying without regrouping

Find 232 × 3.

Hundreds	Tens	Ones
		[dots] [dots]
		[dots] [dots]
		[dots] [dots]
		2 × 3 = 6

Step 1
Multiply the ones by 3.
2 ones × 3 = 6 ones

$$2 \times 3 = 6$$

Step 2
Multiply the tens by 3.
3 tens × 3 = 9 tens

$$2 \times 3 = 6$$
$$30 \times 3 = 90$$

Hundreds	Tens	Ones
	[tens]	[ones]
	[tens]	[ones]
	[tens]	[ones]
	30 × 3 = 90	2 × 3 = 6

Continued on next page

Hundreds	Tens	Ones
$200 \times 3 = 600$	$30 \times 3 = 90$	$2 \times 3 = 6$

Step 3
Multiply the hundreds by 3.
2 hundreds $\times$ 3
$= 6$ hundreds

$$
\begin{aligned}
2 \times 3 &= 6 \\
30 \times 3 &= 90 \\
200 \times 3 &= 600 \\
\text{Total} &= 696
\end{aligned}
$$

Multiplying with regrouping in hundreds, tens, and ones

Find 125×7.

Step 1
Multiply the ones by 7.
5 ones $\times$ 7 $=$ 35 ones
Regroup the ones. 35 ones $=$ 3 tens 5 ones

$$
\begin{array}{r}
\overset{3}{1}\,2\,5 \\
\times \quad 7 \\
\hline
5
\end{array}
$$

Step 2
Multiply the tens by 7.
2 tens $\times$ 7 $=$ 14 tens
Add the tens. 14 tens $+$ 3 tens $=$ 17 tens
Regroup the tens. 17 tens $=$ 1 hundred 7 tens

$$
\begin{array}{r}
\overset{1}{1}\overset{3}{2}\,5 \\
\times \quad 7 \\
\hline
7\,5
\end{array}
$$

Step 3
Multiply the hundreds by 7.
1 hundred $\times$ 7 $=$ 7 hundreds
Add the hundreds. 7 hundreds $+$ 1 hundred $=$ 8 hundreds
So, $125 \times 7 = 875$.

$$
\begin{array}{r}
\overset{1}{1}\overset{3}{2}\,5 \\
\times \quad 7 \\
\hline
8\,7\,5
\end{array}
$$

Dividing with remainders

Find 43 ÷ 5.

43 ones ÷ 5 = 8 ones with remainder
                  3 ones
               = 8 R 3

```
      8 R 3
  5) 4   3
```

First, choose a quotient.
       5 × 8 = 40
40 is less than 43.
       5 × 9 = 45
45 is greater than 43.
       Choose 8.

Quotient   = 8 ones = 8
Remainder = 3 ones = 3

Dividing without remainders and regrouping

Find 84 ÷ 4.

Tens	Ones

Step 1
Divide the tens by 4.
8 tens ÷ 4 = 2 tens

```
     2
 4) 8   4
    8   0
    ─────
        4
```

Continued on next page

Tens	Ones
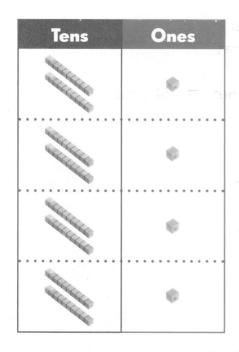

Step 2
Divide the ones by 4.
4 ones ÷ 4 = 1 one

$$\begin{array}{r} 2\ \ \mathbf{1} \\ 4\overline{)8\ \ 4} \\ 8\ \ 0 \\ \hline 4 \\ \mathbf{4} \\ \hline \mathbf{0} \end{array}$$

So, 84 ÷ 4 = 21.

Dividing with regrouping in tens and ones

Find 54 ÷ 3.

Tens	Ones
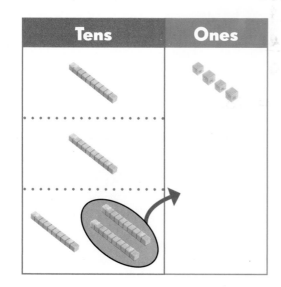

Step 1
Divide the tens by 3.
5 tens ÷ 3 = 1 ten with
                2 tens left over

$$\begin{array}{r} \mathbf{1} \\ 3\overline{)5\ \ 4} \\ \mathbf{3}\ \ 0 \\ \hline \mathbf{2} \end{array}$$

Tens	Ones

Regroup the 2 tens.
2 tens = 20 ones
Add the ones.
4 ones + 20 ones = 24 ones

```
       1
  3) 5  4
     3  0
     2  4
```

Tens	Ones

Step 2
Divide the ones by 3.
24 ones ÷ 3 = 8 ones

```
       1  8
  3) 5  4
     3  0
     2  4
     2  4
        0
```

So, 54 ÷ 3 = 18.

Multiply using repeated addition.

1 4 × 8 = 4 groups of [ ]

= [ ] + [ ] + [ ] + [ ]

= [ ]

2 6 × 9 = 6 groups of [ ]

= [ ] + [ ] + [ ] + [ ] + [ ] + [ ]

= [ ]

Divide using repeated subtraction.

3 15 ÷ 5 = [ ]

15 − [ ] − [ ] − [ ] = 0

4 32 ÷ 8 = [ ]

32 − [ ] − [ ] − [ ] − [ ] = 0

Multiply.

5 6 × 6 = [ ]

6 9 × 4 = [ ]

7 7 × 100 = [ ]

8 320 × 3 = [ ]

9 215 × 3 = [ ]

10 187 × 5 = [ ]

Divide.

11 17 ÷ 3 = [ ]

12 35 ÷ 2 = [ ]

13 86 ÷ 2 = [ ]

14 96 ÷ 4 = [ ]

15 56 ÷ 4 = [ ]

16 72 ÷ 3 = [ ]

Lesson 3.1 Multiplying by a 1-Digit Number

Lesson Objective

- Use different methods to multiply up to 4-digit numbers by 1-digit numbers, with or without regrouping.

Learn **Represent numbers using place-value charts.**

213 can be represented in these ways.

Hundreds	Tens	Ones

Hundreds	Tens	Ones
○ ○	○	○ ○ ○

Hundreds	Tens	Ones
2	1	3

Model multiplication with regrouping in thousands, hundreds, tens, and ones.

Roy's Market sold 2,476 oranges. Ana's Market sold 3 times as many oranges as Roy's Market. How many oranges did Ana's Market sell?

$2,476 \times 3 = ?$

Step 1 Multiply the ones by 3.

$$6 \text{ ones } \times 3 = 18 \text{ ones}$$
$$= 1 \text{ ten } 8 \text{ ones}$$

Thousands	Hundreds	Tens	Ones

```
   Th H T O
          1
    2, 4 7 6
  ×        3
  ─────────
           8
```

Step 2 Multiply the tens by 3.

$$7 \text{ tens } \times 3 = 21 \text{ tens}$$

Add the tens.

$$21 \text{ tens } + 1 \text{ ten } = 22 \text{ tens}$$
$$= 2 \text{ hundreds } 2 \text{ tens}$$

Thousands	Hundreds	Tens	Ones

```
   Th H T O
        2 1
    2, 4 7 6
  ×        3
  ─────────
         2 8
```

Step 3 Multiply the hundreds by 3.

4 hundreds × 3 = 12 hundreds

Add the hundreds.

12 hundreds + 2 hundreds

= 14 hundreds = 1 thousand 4 hundreds

Thousands	Hundreds	Tens	Ones
	● ● ● ● ● ● ● ● ● ● ● ● ● ●	● ●	● ● ● ● ● ● ● ●

$$
\begin{array}{r}
\text{Th H T O}\\
{}^{1}\ {}^{2}\ {}^{1}\\
2,4\ 7\ 6\\
\times\quad\quad 3\\
\hline
4\ 2\ 8
\end{array}
$$

Step 4 Multiply the thousands by 3.

2 thousands × 3 = 6 thousands

Add the thousands.

6 thousands + 1 thousand = 7 thousands

Thousands	Hundreds	Tens	Ones
● ● ● ● ● ● ●	● ● ● ●	● ●	● ● ● ● ● ● ● ●

$$
\begin{array}{r}
\text{Th H T O}\\
{}^{1}\ {}^{2}\ {}^{1}\\
2,4\ 7\ 6\\
\times\quad\quad 3\\
\hline
7,4\ 2\ 8
\end{array}
$$

Ana's Market sold 7,428 oranges.

Guided Practice

Find the missing numbers in each step.

1 The next month, Roy's Market sold 6,139 oranges.
Ana's Market sold 9 times as many oranges as Roy's Market.
How many oranges did Ana's Market sell?

$6,139 \times 9 = ?$

Step 1

9 ones $\times$ 9 = 81 ones

= [   ] tens [   ] one

$$\begin{array}{r} \text{Th} \ \ \text{H} \ \ \text{T} \ \ \text{O} \\ \overset{8}{} \\ 6, \ 1 \ \ 3 \ \ \mathbf{9} \\ \times \quad \quad \quad \mathbf{9} \\ \hline [\ \ ] \end{array}$$

Step 2

3 tens $\times$ 9 = 27 tens
Add the tens.

[   ] tens + [   ] tens

= [   ] tens

= [   ] hundreds [   ] tens

$$\begin{array}{r} \overset{8}{} \\ 6, \ 1 \ \ \mathbf{3} \ \ 9 \\ \times \quad \quad \quad \mathbf{9} \\ \hline [\ ][\ ] \end{array}$$

Step 3

1 hundred $\times$ 9 = 9 hundreds
Add the hundreds.

[   ] hundreds + [   ] hundreds

= [   ] hundreds

= [   ] thousand [   ] hundreds

$$\begin{array}{r} \overset{3}{} \overset{8}{} \\ 6, \ \mathbf{1} \ \ 3 \ \ 9 \\ \times \quad \quad \quad \mathbf{9} \\ \hline [\ ][\ ][\ ] \end{array}$$

Step 4

6 thousands × 9 = 54 thousands

Add the thousands.

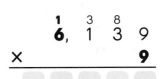

[____] thousands + [____] thousand

= [____] thousands

Ana's Market sold 55,251 oranges.

Multiply. Use place-value charts to help you.

2
```
    1 2 6
  ×     4
```
[____]

3
```
    2 7 8
  ×     7
```
[____]

4
```
  4, 7 1 6
  ×       5
```
[____]

Learn — Multiply using the place value of each digit.

2,147 × 4 = ?

```
      2, 1 4 7
  ×         4
  _____
          2 8   ←——————  7 × 4
  +     1 6 0   ←——————  40 × 4
  +     4 0 0   ←——————  100 × 4
  + 8, 0 0 0   ←—————— 2,000 × 4
  _____
    8, 5 8 8
```

Guided Practice

Multiply using the method shown above.

5
```
    6 7 4
  ×     5
```
[____]

6
```
  8, 0 1 2
  ×       9
```
[____]

7
```
  9, 0 0 9
  ×       9
```
[____]

WORK IN PAIRS ▸ Game

Roll and Multiply!

Players: 2
Materials:
• Chip models
• Number cubes

STEP 1 Player 1 tosses the number cube four times to get a 4-digit number, for example 5,421.

STEP 2 Player 2 tosses the number cube once to get a 1-digit number, for example 6.

$$
\begin{array}{r}
\overset{2\ \ 1}{5,4\,2\,1} \\
\times \qquad 6 \\
\hline
3\,2,5\,2\,6
\end{array}
$$

STEP 3 Player 1 uses the chip model (shown on pages 78 and 79) to multiply the 4-digit number by the 1-digit number.

STEP 4 Then Player 1 writes the answer as shown in the example.

Example

4-Digit Number	1-Digit Number	Product
5,421	6	$5{,}421 \times 6 = 32{,}526$

STEP 5 Player 2 checks the answer. Player 1 gets one point if the answer is correct.

STEP 6 Take turns writing the product and checking the answer. Play three rounds.

The player with the higher score wins!

Example

Look at the steps for multiplying a 3-digit number by a 1-digit number.

$$\begin{array}{r} \overset{1\ 3}{2\ 1\ 5} \\ \times \quad\quad 7 \\ \hline 1,5\,0\,5 \end{array}$$

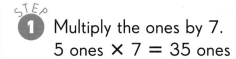

STEP 1 Multiply the ones by 7.
5 ones × 7 = 35 ones

Regroup the ones.
35 ones = 3 tens 5 ones

STEP 2 Multiply the tens by 7.
1 ten × 7 = 7 tens

Add the tens.
7 tens + 3 tens = 10 tens

Regroup the tens.
10 tens = 1 hundred

STEP 3 Multiply the hundreds by 7.
2 hundreds × 7 = 14 hundreds

Add the hundreds.
14 hundreds + 1 hundred = 15 hundreds

Regroup the hundreds.
15 hundreds = 1 thousand 5 hundreds

The product is 1,505.

What are the steps to find the product of 6,875 and 3?

Let's Explore!

WORKING TOGETHER

Three students completed these multiplication problems. Find the errors.

1
$$\begin{array}{r} {\scriptstyle 1\ 3\ 4} \\ 1,2\ 4\ 5 \\ \times\qquad 8 \\ \hline 8,6\ 2\ 0 \end{array}$$

2
$$\begin{array}{r} 6\ 7\ 3 \\ \times\qquad 3 \\ \hline 1\ 8,2\ 1\ 9 \end{array}$$

3
$$\begin{array}{r} {\scriptstyle 1\ 3} \\ 1\ 0\ 3\ 6 \\ \times\qquad 5 \\ \hline 5,5\ 8\ 0 \end{array}$$

Discuss with your classmates some common errors that students make in multiplication.

Let's Practice

Multiply and find the missing numbers.

1 7 ones × 4 = [ ] ones

= [ ] tens [ ] ones

$$\begin{array}{r} 7 \\ \times\quad 4 \\ \hline [\quad] \end{array}$$

2 8 tens × 5 = [ ] tens

= [ ] hundreds [ ] tens

$$\begin{array}{r} 8\ 0 \\ \times\quad 5 \\ \hline [\quad] \end{array}$$

3 6 hundreds × 3 = [ ] hundreds

= [ ] thousand [ ] hundreds

$$\begin{array}{r} 6\ 0\ 0 \\ \times\quad 3 \\ \hline [\quad] \end{array}$$

Multiply and find the missing numbers.

4 9 thousands × 2 = [ ] thousands

= [ ] ten thousand [ ] thousands

$$\begin{array}{r} 9{,}000 \\ \times2 \\ \hline \boxed{} \end{array}$$

Multiply.

5 8 × 3 = [ ]

6 80 × 3 = [ ]

7 800 × 3 = [ ]

8 8,000 × 3 = [ ]

Multiply.

9
$$\begin{array}{r} 104 \\ \times5 \\ \hline \boxed{} \end{array}$$

10
$$\begin{array}{r} 754 \\ \times3 \\ \hline \boxed{} \end{array}$$

11
$$\begin{array}{r} 217 \\ \times8 \\ \hline \boxed{} \end{array}$$

12
$$\begin{array}{r} 9{,}110 \\ \times8 \\ \hline \boxed{} \end{array}$$

13
$$\begin{array}{r} 1{,}026 \\ \times8 \\ \hline \boxed{} \end{array}$$

14
$$\begin{array}{r} 2{,}307 \\ \times3 \\ \hline \boxed{} \end{array}$$

15
$$\begin{array}{r} 4{,}635 \\ \times7 \\ \hline \boxed{} \end{array}$$

16
$$\begin{array}{r} 8{,}319 \\ \times8 \\ \hline \boxed{} \end{array}$$

ON YOUR OWN

Go to Workbook A:
Practice 1, pages 41–44

3.2 Multiplying by a 2-Digit Number

Lesson Objectives

- Multiply by 2-digit numbers, with or without regrouping.
- Estimate products.

Learn **Multiply by tens.**

Kevin packs 4 bags of apples. Each bag contains 10 apples. How many apples does Kevin pack altogether?

$4 \times 10 = ?$

Tens	Ones
●	
●	
●	
●	

$$4 \times 10 = 4 \times 1 \text{ ten}$$
$$= 4 \text{ tens}$$
$$= 40$$

Kevin packs 40 apples altogether.

Rafael buys 3 packages of crayons. Each package contains 20 crayons. How many crayons does Rafael buy?

$3 \times 20 = ?$

Tens	Ones
● ●	
● ●	
● ●	

$$3 \times 20 = 3 \times 2 \text{ tens}$$
$$= 6 \text{ tens}$$
$$= 60$$

Rafael buys 60 crayons.

Guided Practice

Find the missing numbers.

1 14 × 10 = [　　] × [　　] ten = [　　] tens = [　　]

2 7 × 30 = [　　] × [　　] tens = [　　] tens = [　　]

3 9 × 40 = 9 × [　　] tens = [　　] tens = [　　]

4 58 × 60 = [　　] × [　　] tens = [　　] tens = [　　]

5 47 × 80 = [　　] × [　　] tens = [　　] tens = [　　]

Learn Here are two ways to multiply by hundreds.

Find the **product** of 24 and 300.

Method 1

24 × 300 = 24 × 3 × 100
          = 72 × 100
          = 7,200

300 = 3 × 100

Method 2

24 × 300 = 24 × 100 × 3
          = 2,400 × 3
          = 7,200

300 = 100 × 3

Guided Practice

Find the missing numbers.

6 $43 \times 50 = 43 \times \boxed{} \times 5 = \boxed{} \times 5 = \boxed{}$

7 $216 \times 30 = 216 \times \boxed{} \times 10 = \boxed{} \times 10 = \boxed{}$

8 $37 \times 200 = 37 \times \boxed{} \times 100 = \boxed{} \times 100 = \boxed{}$

9 $75 \times 800 = 75 \times \boxed{} \times 8 = \boxed{} \times 8 = \boxed{}$

Multiply.

10 $32 \times 10 = \boxed{}$ **11** $457 \times 10 = \boxed{}$ **12** $93 \times 30 = \boxed{}$

13 $210 \times 20 = \boxed{}$ **14** $41 \times 500 = \boxed{}$ **15** $68 \times 800 = \boxed{}$

Learn Multiply a 2-digit number by a 2-digit number.

Midtown Gardens has 27 barrels filled with rainwater.
Each barrel contains 32 liters of water.
What is the total amount of water in the barrels?

$27 \times 32 = ?$

Step 1

Multiply 2 tens 7 ones by 2.

7 ones $\times$ 2 = 14 ones
$\qquad\qquad$ = 1 ten 4 ones

2 tens $\times$ 2 = 4 tens

Add.

4 tens $+$ 1 ten 4 ones = 5 tens 4 ones

Part of the product: $27 \times 2 = 54$

$$\begin{array}{r} {\scriptstyle 1} \\ 2\,\mathbf{7} \\ \times\ \ 3\,\mathbf{2} \\ \hline 5\,4 \end{array}$$

Step 2

Multiply 2 tens 7 ones by 30.

7 ones × 30 = 210 ones
      = 21 tens
      = 2 hundreds 1 ten

2 tens × 30 = 60 tens
       = 6 hundreds

Add.

6 hundreds + 2 hundreds 1 ten = 8 hundreds 1 ten

Part of the product: 27 × 30 = 810

```
      2
      1
      2 7
  ×   3 2
      5 4
    8 1 0
```

Step 3

Add the two parts of the product.

54 + 810 = 864

27 × 32 = 864

The total amount of water is 864 liters.

```
      2
      1
      2 7
  ×   3 2
      5 4
    8 1 0
    8 6 4
```

Guided Practice

Find each product.

16
```
    6 2
  × 1 5
```

17
```
    4 6
  × 5 8
```

18
```
    8 7
  × 3 9
```

Learn

Multiply a 3-digit number by a 2-digit number.

Mrs. Wong earns $315 in one week. How much does she earn in 23 weeks?

Step 1

Multiply 3 hundreds 1 ten 5 ones by 3.

$$5 \text{ ones} \times 3 = 15 \text{ ones}$$
$$= 1 \text{ ten } 5 \text{ ones}$$
$$1 \text{ ten} \times 3 = 3 \text{ tens}$$
$$3 \text{ hundreds} \times 3 = 9 \text{ hundreds}$$

Add.

9 hundreds + 3 tens + 1 ten 5 ones
= 9 hundreds 4 tens 5 ones

Part of the product: $315 \times 3 = 945$

```
      1
    3 1 5
  ×   2 3
    9 4 5
```

Step 2

Multiply 3 hundreds 1 ten 5 ones by 20.

$$5 \text{ ones} \times 20 = 100 \text{ ones}$$
$$= 10 \text{ tens}$$
$$= 1 \text{ hundred}$$
$$1 \text{ ten} \times 20 = 20 \text{ tens}$$
$$= 2 \text{ hundreds}$$
$$3 \text{ hundreds} \times 20 = 60 \text{ hundreds}$$
$$= 6 \text{ thousands}$$

Add.

6 thousands + 2 hundreds + 1 hundred
= 6 thousands 3 hundreds

Part of the product: $315 \times 20 = 6,300$

```
      1
      1
    3 1 5
  ×   2 3
    9 4 5
  6,3 0 0
```

Step 3

Add the two parts of the product.

$$945 + 6,300 = 7,245$$

$$315 \times 23 = 7,245$$

Mrs. Wong earns $7,245 in 23 weeks.

```
      1
    3 1 5
  ×   2 3
    9 4 5
  6,3 0 0
  7,2 4 5
```

Guided Practice

Multiply.

19
```
    3 7 9
×     2 2
```

20
```
    9 3 7
×     1 6
```

21
```
    6 0 5
×     4 8
```

WORK IN PAIRS **Game**

Players: 2

Find the Missing Numbers!

STEP 1 Player 1 writes a multiplication problem with a 2-digit number multiplied by a 2-digit number.

STEP 2 Player 1 finds the answer and then replaces any 3 digits in the solution with boxes, on a new sheet of paper.

Example

```
      4 3
×     3 5
      2 1 5
    1, 2 9 0
    1, 5 0 5
```

```
      4 3
×     3 5
    [2] 1 5
    1, 2 [9] 0  } solution
    1, [5] 0 5
```

STEP 3 Player 2 then fills in the missing numbers in the boxes.

STEP 4 Player 1 checks the answer. Player 2 gets one point for each correct number in the boxes.

STEP 5 Take turns writing the problem and checking the answer. Play three rounds.

· ·
The player with the higher score wins!
· ·

Learn **Use a number line to estimate products.**

Estimate 23 × 59.

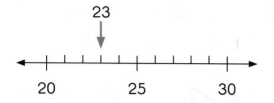

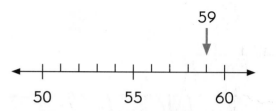

23 is closer to 20 than to 30.

59 is closer to 60 than to 50.

20 × 60 = 1,200
23 × 59 is about 1,200.

Round

23 × 59

↓   ↓

20   60

Guided Practice

Use a number line to estimate the product.

22 Estimate the product of 38 × 715.

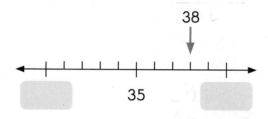

35

38 is closer to [ ] than to [ ].

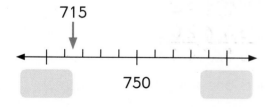

750

715 is closer to [ ] than to [ ].

[ ] × [ ] = [ ]

38 × 715 is about [ ].

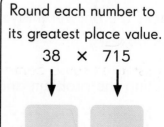

Round each number to
its greatest place value.

38 × 715

↓   ↓

[ ]   [ ]

Multiply. Then estimate to check that your answers are reasonable.
Round each number to its greatest place value.

23 68 × 94 = ☐

Estimate: ☐

24 489 × 27 = ☐

Estimate: ☐

Let's Explore!

WORKING TOGETHER

Work in groups of four.

Ryan got these multiplication problems wrong in a test. Find his errors in each problem and then show the correct answer.

1
```
      2 5 9
  ×     6 2
      4 1 8
  1 5, 5 4 0
  1 5, 9 5 8
```

2
```
        5 7
  ×     3 3
      1 7 1
      1 7 1
      3 4 2
```

3
```
      3 6 5
  ×     8 6
    2, 1 9 0
    2, 9 2 0
    5, 1 1 0
```

4
```
      7 0 8
  ×     9 3
    2, 1 2 4
  6 3, 6 2 0
  6 5, 7 4 4
```

Discuss with your classmates some common errors that students make in multiplication.

Let's Practice

Find the missing numbers.

1 86 ×ʹ 40 = [ ]

2 60 × 59 = [ ]

3 47 × 500 = [ ]

4 300 × 94 = [ ]

Multiply.

5
```
    2 5
×   7 5
```
[ ]

6
```
      8 9
×     4 6
```
[ ]

7
```
    7 0 5
×     3 6
```
[ ]

8
```
    9 1 5
×     1 8
```
[ ]

Use the number line to estimate the product.

9 47 × 53

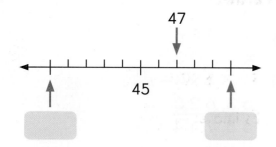

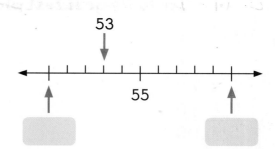

47 is closer to [ ] than to [ ].　　　53 is closer to [ ] than to [ ].

[ ] × [ ] = [ ].

47 × 53 is about [ ].

Estimate each product.

Round each number to its greatest place value.

10 76 × 249 is about [ ] × [ ]

= [ ]

11 33 × 84 is about [ ] × [ ]

= [ ]

12 23 × 415 is about [ ] × 400

= [ ]

13 33 × 278 is about 30 × [ ]

= [ ]

14 52 × 536 is about [ ] × [ ]

= [ ]

15 139 × 75 is about [ ] × [ ]

= [ ]

16 462 × 53 is about [ ] × [ ]

= [ ]

Multiply. Then estimate to check that your answers are reasonable.

Round each number to its greatest place value.

17 64 × 92 = [ ]

Estimate: [ ]

18 71 × 839 = [ ]

Estimate: [ ]

19 389 × 64 = [ ]

Estimate: [ ]

ON YOUR OWN

**Go to Workbook A:
Practice 2, pages 45–48**

Lesson 3.3 Modeling Division with Regrouping

Lesson Objectives

- Model regrouping in division.
- Divide a 3-digit number by a 1-digit number with regrouping.

Vocabulary
regroup

Learn Model division with regrouping in hundreds, tens, and ones.

A farmer sells his crops to 3 restaurants. He divides 525 heads of lettuce equally among the 3 restaurants. How many heads of lettuce does each restaurant receive?

$525 \div 3 = ?$

Hundreds	Tens	Ones
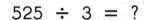		

Step 1

Divide the hundreds by 3.

5 hundreds ÷ 3 = 1 hundred with 2 hundreds left over

```
      1
  3) 5 2 5
     3 0 0
     2
```

Hundreds	Tens	Ones

Regroup the hundreds.

2 hundreds = 20 tens

Add the tens.

20 tens + 2 tens = 22 tens

```
      1
  3) 5 2 5
     3 0 0
     2 2 5
```

Hundreds	Tens	Ones

Step 2
Divide the tens by 3.

22 tens ÷ 3 = 7 tens
with 1 ten left over

```
      1  7
  3)  5  2  5
      3  0  0
      2  2  5
      2  1  0
            1
```

Regroup the ten.
1 ten = 10 ones

Add the ones.
10 ones + 5 ones = 15 ones

```
      1  7
  3)  5  2  5
      3  0  0
      2  2  5
      2  1  0
         1  5
```

Step 3
Divide the ones by 3.

15 ones ÷ 3 = 5 ones

```
      1  7  5
  3)  5  2  5
      3  0  0
      2  2  5
      2  1  0
         1  5
         1  5
            0
```

So, 525 ÷ 3 = 175.
Each restaurant receives 175 heads of lettuce.

Guided Practice

Complete each step.

1 The farmer divides 735 carrots equally among 3 restaurants. How many carrots does each restaurant receive?

$735 \div 3 = ?$

Hundreds	Tens	Ones
● ●	● ● ●	● ● ●
		● ●
● ●		
● ●		

↓

Hundreds	Tens	Ones
● ●	● ● ●	
	● ● ●	
● ●	● ●	
	● ● ●	
● ●	● ●	

Step 1
Divide the hundreds by 3.

```
        2
   3) 7 3 5
      6 0 0
      1
```

7 hundreds ÷ 3 = ⬚ hundreds with ⬚ hundred left over

Regroup the hundred.

⬚ hundred = ⬚ tens

Add the tens.

⬚ tens + ⬚ tens

= ⬚ tens

```
        2
   3) 7 3 5
      6 0 0
      1 3 5
```

Hundreds	Tens	Ones

(Place value chart showing hundreds, tens, and ones with an arrow regrouping a ten to ones)

↓

Hundreds	Tens	Ones

Hundreds	Tens	Ones

So, 735 ÷ 3 = [ ] .

Each restaurant receives [ ] carrots.

Step 2
Divide the tens by 3.

```
      2   4
  3) 7  3  5
     6  0  0
     1  3  5
     1  2  0
           1
```

[ ] tens ÷ 3 = [ ] tens

with [ ] ten left over

Regroup the ten.

[ ] ten = [ ] ones

Add the ones.

[ ] ones + [ ] ones

= [ ] ones

```
      2   4
  3) 7  3  5
     6  0  0
     1  3  5
     1  2  0
        1  5
```

Step 3
Divide the ones by 3.

[ ] ones ÷ 3 = [ ] ones

```
      2   4   5
  3) 7  3  5
     6  0  0
     1  3  5
     1  2  0
        1  5
        1  5
           0
```

Find the missing numbers.

2 $578 \div 2 = \boxed{}$

$$2\overline{)5\ 7\ 8}$$ → $$2\overline{)5\ 7\ 8}$$ ... 7 → $$2\overline{)5\ 7\ 8}$$ ... 7 → $$2\overline{)5\ 7\ 8}$$ ... 7 ... 8 ... 0

Divide.

3 $338 \div 2 = \boxed{}$

4 $345 \div 5 = \boxed{}$

5 $656 \div 4 = \boxed{}$

6 $138 \div 3 = \boxed{}$

7 Mr. Young has 256 stickers. He gives each of his 8 grandchildren an equal number of stickers. How many stickers does each grandchild get?

Let's Practice

Divide.

1 $267 \div 3 = \boxed{}$

2 $528 \div 4 = \boxed{}$

3 $465 \div 5 = \boxed{}$

4 $714 \div 7 = \boxed{}$

5 $837 \div 9 = \boxed{}$

6 $952 \div 8 = \boxed{}$

ON YOUR OWN

Go to Workbook A:
Practice 3, pages 49–54

Lesson 3.4 Dividing by a 1-Digit Number

Lesson Objectives

- Divide up to a 4-digit number by a 1-digit number with regrouping, and with or without remainders.
- Estimate quotients.

Vocabulary
quotient
remainder

Learn Divide with no remainder.

Find 10 ÷ 5.

10 ÷ 5 = 2

Quotient = 2

Remainder = 0

A **quotient** is the answer to a division problem.
A **remainder** is the number left over when a number cannot be divided evenly.

Learn Divide with a remainder.

$$\begin{array}{r} \mathbf{2} \\ 5\overline{)\,1\;\;3} \\ \underline{\mathbf{1\;\;0}} \\ \mathbf{3} \end{array}$$

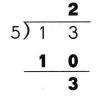

When dividing 13 by 5, you can group 13 into 2 groups of 5 with 3 left over. The number 2 is the quotient, and the remainder is 3.

Divide by a 1-digit number with no remainder.

At a carnival, 6,381 apples are given out to children.
Each child receives 3 apples.
How many children are at the carnival?

Step 1
Divide 6 thousands by 3.
6 thousands ÷ 3 = 2 thousands
$\qquad\qquad$ = 2,000

```
      Th  H   T   O
       2
   3) 6 , 3   8   1
      6 , 0   0   0  ← 2,000 × 3
```

Step 2
Divide 3 hundreds by 3.
3 hundreds ÷ 3 = 1 hundred
$\qquad\qquad$ = 100

```
       2   1
   3) 6 , 3   8   1
      6 , 0   0   0
          3   8   1
          3   0   0  ← 100 × 3
```

Step 3
Divide 8 tens by 3.
8 tens ÷ 3 = 2 tens with 2 tens left over
$\qquad\qquad$ = 20 with 20 left over

```
       2   1   2
   3) 6 , 3   8   1
      6 , 0   0   0
          3   8   1
          3   0   0
              8   1
              6   0  ← 20 × 3
              2   1
```

Step 4
Divide 21 ones by 3.
21 ones ÷ 3 = 7 ones
$\qquad\qquad$ = 7

```
       2 , 1   2   7  ← quotient
   3) 6 , 3   8   1
      6 , 0   0   0
          3   8   1
          3   0   0
              8   1
              6   0
              2   1
              2   1  ← 7 × 3
                  0  ← remainder
```

When 6,381 is divided by 3, the quotient
is 2,127 and the remainder is 0.

There are 2,127 children at the carnival.

Guided Practice

Find the missing numbers.

1 Divide 6,144 by 6.

Step 1
Divide 6 thousands by 6.
6 thousands ÷ 6 = ☐ thousand = ☐

Step 2
Divide 1 hundred by 6.
1 hundred ÷ 6 = ☐ hundreds with

☐ hundred left over

= ☐ with ☐ left over

Step 3
Divide 14 tens by 6.
14 tens ÷ 6 = ☐ tens with ☐ tens left over

= ☐ with ☐ left over

Step 4
Divide 24 ones by 6.
24 ones ÷ 6 = ☐ ones

= ☐

When 6,144 is divided by 6, the quotient is ☐.

	Th	H	T	O
6)	6,	1	4	4
	6,	**0**	**0**	**0**

	Th	H	T	O
6)	6,	1	4	4
	6,	0	0	0
		1	4	4
		0	0	0

	Th	H	T	O
6)	6,	1	4	4
	6,	0	0	0
		1	4	4
		0	0	0
		1	4	4
		1	**2**	0
			2	4

	Th	H	T	O
6)	6,	1	4	4
	6,	0	0	0
		1	4	4
		0	0	0
		1	4	4
		1	2	0
			2	4
			2	**4**

Divide.

2 $\quad$ 6$\overline{)1,536}$

3 $\quad$ 4$\overline{)7,216}$

Learn **Find the quotient and the remainder.**

Divide 2,634 by 4.

```
        6
   4)2, 6  3  4
   2, 4  0  0
      2  3  4
```

```
        6  5
   4)2, 6  3  4
   2, 4  0  0
      2  3  4
      2  0  0
         3  4
```

```
        6  5  8  ←  quotient
   4)2, 6  3  4
   2, 4  0  0
      2  3  4
      2  0  0
         3  4
         3  2
            2  ←  remainder
```

When 2,634 is divided by 4, the quotient
is 658 and the remainder is 2.

Guided Practice

Find the quotient and the remainder.

4 $\quad$ Divide 6,100 by 8.

```
   8)6, 1  0  0
   5, 6  0  0
      5  0  0
```

```
   8)6, 1  0  0
   5, 6  0  0
      5  0  0
      4  8  0
         2  0
```

```
   8)6, 1  0  0
   5, 6  0  0
      5  0  0
      4  8  0
         2  0
         1  6
```

When 6,100 is divided by 8, the quotient is [   ]
and the remainder is [   ].

Divide. Find each quotient (Q) and remainder (R).

5 5,608 ÷ 6

Q = [ ]   R = [ ]

6 2,117 ÷ 7

Q = [ ]   R = [ ]

7 4,135 ÷ 3

Q = [ ]   R = [ ]

8 4,165 ÷ 5

Q = [ ]   R = [ ]

9 3,796 ÷ 9

Q = [ ]   R = [ ]

10 5,084 ÷ 7

Q = [ ]   R = [ ]

Find each quotient and remainder.

11
$$4\overline{)423}$$

12
$$9\overline{)1,803}$$

Estimate quotients using related multiplication facts.

Find 438 ÷ 5.

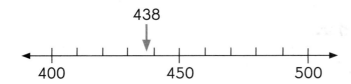

438

400   450   500

Related multiplication facts:
5 × 8 = 40   5 × 9 = 45
438 ÷ 5 is about 450 ÷ 5.
The estimated quotient is 90.

5 × 80 = 400
5 × 90 = 450
438 is closer to
450 than to 400.

Guided Practice

Estimate each quotient.

13 83 ÷ 2 is about [ ] ÷ 2

= [ ]

14 96 ÷ 5 is about [ ] ÷ 5

= [ ]

15 865 ÷ 3 is about [ ] ÷ 3

= [ ]

16 586 ÷ 6 is about [ ] ÷ 6

= [ ]

17 269 ÷ 6 is about [ ] ÷ 6

= [ ]

18 2,079 ÷ 7 is about [ ] ÷ 7

= [ ]

19 764 ÷ 8 is about [ ] ÷ 8

= [ ]

20 7,175 ÷ 9 is about [ ] ÷ 9

= [ ]

21 47 ÷ 5 is about [ ] ÷ 5

= [ ]

22 383 ÷ 4 is about [ ] ÷ 4

= [ ]

23 617 ÷ 6 is about [ ] ÷ 6

= [ ]

24 3,555 ÷ 9 is about [ ] ÷ 9

= [ ]

Divide. Then estimate to check that your answers are reasonable.

25 7,146 ÷ 7

[ ]

7) 7,146

Estimate:

[ ] ÷ 7 = [ ]

7,146 ÷ 7 is about [ ].

26 6,351 ÷ 8

[ ]

8) 6,351

Estimate:

[ ] ÷ 8 = [ ]

6,351 ÷ 8 is about [ ].

Divide. Then estimate to check that your answers are reasonable.

 27 617 ÷ 6

28 6,369 ÷ 8

 29 5,058 ÷ 5

30 6,702 ÷ 7

 Let's Explore!

WORKING TOGETHER

Four students, Allen, Ben, Carol, and Dawn, solved this problem.

Estimate the quotient of 468 ÷ 5.

These are the answers they got.
Allen   2,500   Ben   450
Carol   90   Dawn 9
Discuss with your classmates how they got their answers.
Explain which of the answers are unreasonable.

Let's Practice

Complete the missing number to find each quotient.

1 8,000 ÷ 4 = [   ] thousands ÷ 4 = [   ] thousands = [   ]

2 9,000 ÷ 3 = [   ] thousands ÷ 3 = [   ] thousands = [   ]

3 1,200 ÷ 6 = [   ] hundreds ÷ 6 = [   ] hundreds = [   ]

4 1,500 ÷ 5 = [   ] hundreds ÷ 5 = [   ] hundreds = [   ]

Divide.

5 [ ]

8$\overline{)9,968}$

6 [ ]

5$\overline{)6,850}$

Find each quotient and remainder.

7 9 tens ÷ 4

Quotient = [ ]

Remainder = [ ]

8 24 ones ÷ 5

Quotient = [ ]

Remainder = [ ]

9 15 hundreds ÷ 6

Quotient = [ ]

Remainder = [ ]

10 12 thousands ÷ 7

Quotient = [ ]

Remainder = [ ]

Find each quotient (Q) and remainder (R).

11 5,235 ÷ 5

Q = [ ]   R = [ ]

12 3,581 ÷ 8

Q = [ ]   R = [ ]

Find each quotient and remainder.

13 [ ]

4$\overline{)713}$

14 [ ]

9$\overline{)1,708}$

Use related multiplication facts to estimate each quotient.

15 92 ÷ 5 is about [ ] ÷ 5

= [ ]

16 791 ÷ 4 is about [ ] ÷ 4

= [ ]

17 6,925 ÷ 7 is about [ ] ÷ 7

= [ ]

18 4,630 ÷ 8 is about [ ] ÷ 8

= [ ]

Divide. Then estimate to check that your answers are reasonable.

19 2,826 ÷ 9 [ ]

20 9,528 ÷ 8 [ ]

ON YOUR OWN

Go to Workbook A:
Practice 4, pages 55–58

Real-World Problems: Multiplication and Division

Lesson Objective

- Solve real-world problems.

Learn **Solve 3-step problems using models.**

Mr. Benson and Mr. McKenzie have $4,686 altogether.
Mr. Benson's share is twice as much as Mr. McKenzie's.

a How much is Mr. McKenzie's share?

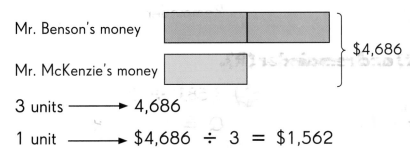

3 units ⟶ 4,686

1 unit ⟶ $4,686 ÷ 3 = $1,562

Mr. McKenzie's share is $1,562.

b How much is Mr. Benson's share?

$1,562 × 2 = $3,124

Mr. Benson's share is $3,124.

c If Mr. Benson spends $500 on books,
how much money does he have left?

$3,124 − $500 = $2,624

Mr. Benson has $2,624 left.

Work backward to check that the
answer for Mr. McKenzie's share is
reasonable. 1,562 is about 1,600.
1,600 × 3 = 4,800
4,800 is close to 4,686.
So, the answer 1,562 is reasonable.

Guided Practice

Solve. Show your work.

1 Mrs. Romero has $3,756 to spend on equipment for the school media room. She saves $650 for later purchases. She spends the rest on 12 monitors and some software. The monitors cost $205 each. How much does she spend on software?

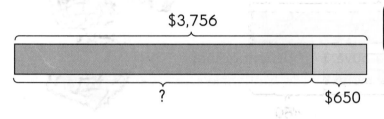

$3,756

? $650

Find the total amount Mrs. Romero spends.

$3,756 − $650 = $3,106
She spends $3,106 altogether.

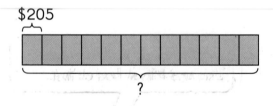

$205

?

Next, find the total cost of 12 monitors.

12 × $205 = $ ☐

The 12 monitors cost $ ☐ .

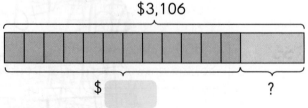

$3,106

$ ☐   ?

Then, subtract the cost of 12 monitors from the total amount Mrs. Romero spends.

$3,106 − $ ☐ = $ ☐

She spends $ ☐ on software.

Learn Solve 3-step problems using models.

Lisa had 1,750 stamps. Minah had 480 fewer stamps than Lisa.
Lisa gave some stamps to Minah.
Now, Minah has 3 times as many stamps as Lisa.

(a) How many stamps did Minah have at first?

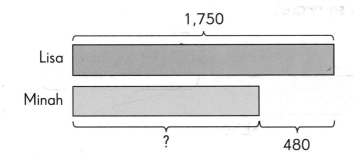

$1,750 - 480 = 1,270$
Minah had 1,270 stamps.

(b) How many stamps does Lisa have now?

$1,750 + 1,270 = 3,020$

> Find the total number of stamps Lisa and Minah had at first.

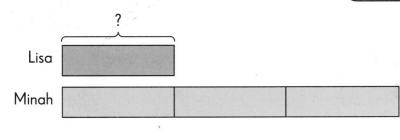

4 units ⟶ 3,020

1 unit ⟶ $3,020 \div 4 = 755$

Lisa has 755 stamps now.

Guided Practice

Solve. Show your work.

2 Ms. Spinelli had $1,240 in her savings account. Her dad had $4,730 in his savings account. Ms. Spinelli's dad transferred some money from his account to her account. Now Ms. Spinelli has twice as much money in her account as her dad does.

a How much money does Ms. Spinelli's dad have now?

$1,240 $4,730

```
┌────────┬──────────────────────┐
│        │                      │
└────────┴──────────────────────┘
```
?

First, find the total amount of money Ms. Spinelli and her dad had.

$ [   ] + $ [   ] = $ [   ]

Ms. Spinelli and her dad had $ [   ] altogether.

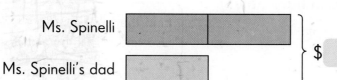

Ms. Spinelli

Ms. Spinelli's dad

$ [   ]

$ [   ] ÷ 3 = $ [   ]

Ms. Spinelli's dad has $ [   ] now.

b How much money did Ms. Spinelli's dad give her?

$4,730 − $ [   ] = $ [   ]

Ms. Spinelli's dad gave her $ [   ].

3 Tim and Ali had 96 marbles altogether.
Tim loses 24 marbles to Ali during a game.
Now, Ali has twice as many marbles as Tim.
How many marbles did Ali have before the game?

After the game:

Ali

Tim

3 units ⟶

1 unit ⟶   ÷ 3 =

2 units ⟶ 2 ×   =

First, find the number of marbles Ali had after the game.

Ali has   marbles after the game.

Before the game:

         − 24 =

Ali had   marbles before the game.

Write real-world multiplication problems using the words and numbers given.
Then solve the problems.

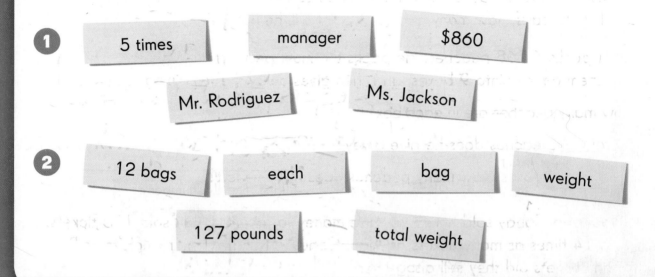

1 | 5 times | manager | $860 |

Mr. Rodriguez   Ms. Jackson

2 | 12 bags | each | bag | weight |

127 pounds   total weight

🔍 Let's Explore!

1 Mrs. Soong and Mrs. Nathan often meet each other in a local market.
Mrs. Soong goes to the market every 2 days and Mrs. Nathan goes to
the market every 3 days. Both of them meet at the market
on January 1 of a calendar year. List the next four dates
on which they will meet again at the market.

Use a calendar
to help you.

2 Look at the dates on which they meet at the market.
Find the pattern. Use the pattern to find four other dates
on which they will meet.

Let's Practice

Solve. Show your work.

1 A store owner buys 1,257 cans of paint. Each can holds 4 quarts of paint. If he sells 620 cans, how many quarts of paint will he have left?

2 A grower packs 4,568 peaches. He packs the most peaches possible, dividing them equally into 9 boxes, and then gives away the remaining peaches.

   a How many peaches are in each box?

   b How many peaches does he give away?

   c If he sells 7 boxes, how many peaches does he have left?

3 Alan, Bob, and Candy sold tickets to raise money for charity. Alan sold 125 tickets. Bob sold 14 times as many tickets as Alan. Candy sold half as many tickets as Bob. How many tickets did they sell altogether?

4 Sam runs laps around a rectangular field 4 times a week. The field is 320 meters long and 240 meters wide. He runs 6 laps each time. What distance does he run in a week?

5 Maya and Emily were playing a board game. Maya had $2,740 in play money and Emily had $3,560. Maya had to give some play money to Emily. After that, Emily had 4 times the amount of play money as Maya.

   a How much money did Maya have in the end?

   b How much money did Emily have in the end?

6 Mr. Rossi has two accounts, Account A and Account B. He had $2,370 in Account B and a total of $7,480 in both accounts. He transferred some money from Account B to Account A. In the end, the amount of money in Account A is 3 times the amount of money in Account B.

   a How much money is there in Account A in the end?

   b How much money did Mr. Rossi transfer from Account B to Account A?

ON YOUR OWN

Go to Workbook A: Practice 5, pages 59–64

CRITICAL THINKING SKILLS
Put On Your Thinking Cap!

PROBLEM SOLVING

Which two numbers below give each product?

12	865

470	45

Use estimation to help you.

1 540

2 5,640

3 38,925

4 21,150

Solve.

5 At a stadium, the number of men is 3 times the number of women. The number of women is 5 times the number of children at the stadium.

 a How many times the number of children is the number of men?

 b If there are 730 children, how many men are there?

6 Kartik places 4 posts along the width of a rectangular garden as shown. The space between two posts is 125 centimeters. He places 10 posts in a similar pattern along the length of the garden. What is the perimeter of the garden?

}125 cm

ON YOUR OWN

**Go to Workbook A:
Put on Your Thinking Cap!
pages 65–66**

Chapter Wrap Up

Study Guide
You have learned...

BIG IDEAS

▶ Place value is used to multiply and divide multi-digit numbers.
▶ Estimation can be used to check the reasonableness of an answer.

Whole Number Multiplication and Division

Multiplication

- Multiply a 4-digit number by a 1-digit number.
- Multiply a 2-digit number by a 2-digit number.
- Multiply a 3-digit number by a 2-digit number.

- Estimate the product by rounding the numbers to the nearest ten or hundred.

 Example
 2,520 × 2 is about 2,500 × 2.
 2,500 × 2 = 5,000

 53 × 28 is about 50 × 30.
 50 × 30 = 1,500

 709 × 42 is about 700 × 40.
 700 × 40 = 28,000

Division

- Model division with regrouping in hundreds, tens, and ones, with or without a remainder.
- Divide a 3-digit number by a 1-digit number with regrouping.
- Divide a 4-digit number by a 1-digit number, with or without a remainder.

- Estimate the quotient by recalling related multiplication facts.

 Example
 7,400 ÷ 8

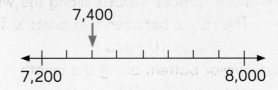

 8 × 900   = 7,200
 8 × 1,000 = 8,000
 7,400 is closer to 7,200 than to 8,000.
 The estimated quotient is 900.

Solve Real-World Problems

Chapter Review/Test

Vocabulary

Choose the correct word.

regroup
remainder
quotient
estimate
rounded
product

1 The number left over when a number cannot be divided evenly is the [   ].

2 When a number is expressed to the nearest ten or hundred, it is [   ].

3 The answer to a division problem is called a [   ].

4 A number close to the exact amount is an [   ].

5 The answer to a multiplication problem is the [   ].

Concepts and Skills
Multiply.

6 $2,755 \times 4 =$ [   ]

7 $48 \times 19 =$ [   ]

8 $485 \times 54 =$ [   ]

Divide.

9 $723 \div 3 =$ [   ]

10 $1,800 \div 6 =$ [   ]

11 $1,968 \div 8 =$ [   ]

Multiply. Then estimate to check that your answers are reasonable.

12 6,964 × 7 = ▢

Estimate: ▢

13 809 × 90 = ▢

Estimate: ▢

Divide. Then estimate to check that your answers are reasonable.

14 623 ÷ 7 = ▢

Estimate: ▢

15 3,627 ÷ 9 = ▢

Estimate: ▢

Problem Solving

Solve. Show your work.

16 A factory produces 9,236 computers. It sells 5,630 computers.
The remaining computers are either damaged or donated to charity.
The number of donated computers is twice the number
of damaged computers.
How many computers are donated to charity?

4 Tables and Line Graphs

Number of Visitors at the Beach

Look at this newspaper article. A bar graph is used to show how many people came to the beach last week.

There seem to be more people visiting the beach on the weekend.

Lessons

4.1 Making and Interpreting a Table

4.2 Using a Table

4.3 Line Graphs

BIG IDEA

▶ Graphs and tables are visual tools for showing and analyzing data.

Recall Prior Knowledge

Reading numbers from a number line

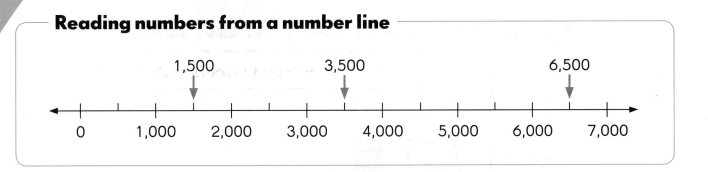

Finding parts and wholes

The tables show the number of boys and girls in two classes.

Ms. Rodger's Class

Number of Boys	Number of Girls	Total
18	24	

$$18 + 24 = 42$$

You can find the whole by adding the parts.

Mr. Tuzimato's Class

Number of Boys	Number of Girls	Total
18		40

$$40 - 18 = 22$$

You can find one part by subtracting the other part from the whole.

Interpreting data in a tally chart

The tally chart shows the number of students born in the months January through June.

Birthday Months of Students

Birthday Month	Number of Students
January	////
February	//// /
March	////
April	//// //
May	//// /
June	//// ////

The greatest number of students were born in June.
The same number of students were born in February and May.
The total number of students in this survey is 37.

Interpreting data in a picture graph

The picture graph shows the number of toy cars each student has.

Number of Toy Cars

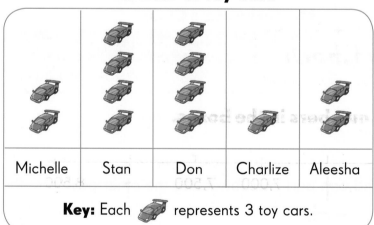

Key: Each 🚗 represents 3 toy cars.

Aleesha has 6 toy cars.
Charlize has the fewest toy cars.
Stan has 12 toy cars. He has the same number of toy cars as Don.
Michelle has 6 fewer toy cars than Stan.

Interpreting data in a bar graph

The bar graph shows the number of visitors at an art show over five days.

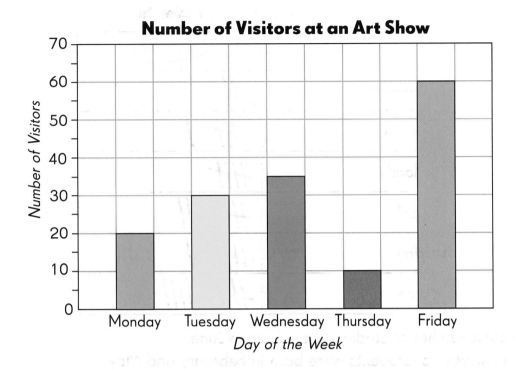

Number of Visitors at an Art Show

The number of visitors at the art show was greatest on Friday.
The number of visitors at the art show was least on Thursday.
There were 25 fewer visitors on Wednesday than on Friday.
There were 20 more visitors on Tuesday than on Thursday.

✔ Quick Check

Find the missing numbers in the boxes.

1

5,500   6,000   7,000   7,500   8,500

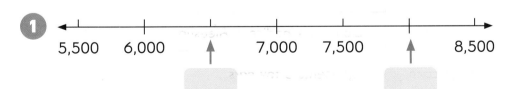

Find the parts and wholes.

2 **Number of Vehicles in a Parking Lot**

Cars	Motorcycles	Total
32	15	

3 **Number of People in a School**

Students	Teachers	Total
	63	1,342

Use the data in the picture graph to complete the tally chart.

The picture graph shows the favorite sports of a group of students.

Favourite Sports of a Group of Students

| Football | Baseball | Basketball | Tennis |

Key: Each ☺ represents 2 students.

Favorite Sports of a Group of Students

Sport	Number of Students
Football	
Baseball	
Basketball	
Tennis	

Complete. Use the data in the tally chart.

4 How many students are fans of basketball?

5 Which sport do the greatest number of students prefer?

6 How many more students prefer basketball to tennis?

7 There are _____ students altogether.

Complete. Use the data in the bar graph.

The bar graph shows the number of fundraising tickets sold by some volunteers.

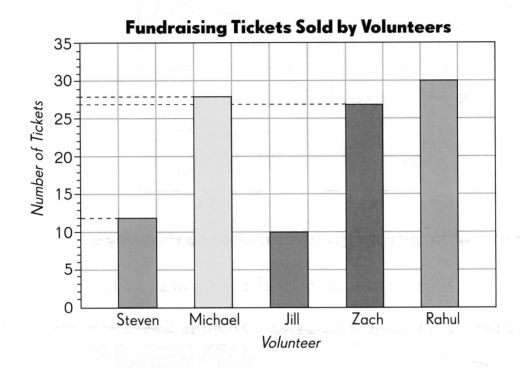

Fundraising Tickets Sold by Volunteers

8 Who sold the greatest number of tickets?

9 Who sold the least number of tickets?

10 How many fewer tickets did Steven sell than Rahul?

11 Which two volunteers sold a difference of 1 ticket?

12 How many tickets did the five volunteers sell altogether?

Making and Interpreting a Table

Lesson Objectives

- Collect, organize, and interpret data in a table.
- Create a table from data in a tally chart and a bar graph.

> **Vocabulary**
> data   table
> tally chart

Learn **Use tables to organize and present data.**

These cards show the names and birthday months of Raul and his friends. They were all born in the same year.

Name: **Raul**
Birthday Month: **March**

Name: **Max**
Birthday Month: **January**

Name: **Olivia**
Birthday Month: **March**

Name: **Dave**
Birthday Month: **March**

Name: **Kwan**

Birthday Month: **April**

Name: **Paula**

Birthday Month: **May**

Name: **Leo**

Birthday Month: **May**

Name: **Wendy**

Birthday Month: **February**

Raul presented the data like this:

Birthday Months of Raul's Friends

Names	Birthday Month
Raul	March
Max	January
Olivia	March
Dave	March
Kwan	April
Paula	May
Leo	May
Wendy	February

Continued on next page

Raul then used a **tally chart** to record what he had found.

Birthday Months of Raul's Friends

Birthday Month	January	February	March	April	May
Tally	/	/	///	/	//

Raul counted the tally marks to find the number of friends whose birthdays fell in each month. Then he presented the data in a table.

Birthday Months of Raul's Friends

Birthday Month	Number of Friends
January	1
February	1
March	3
April	1
May	2

2 of Raul's friends were born in May.
The month with the most number of birthdays is March.
There were 2 more friends born in March than in January.
Raul collected data from 7 friends in total, excluding himself.

Guided Practice

Raul asked each of his friends to bring one type of food for a picnic. He then used a tally chart to record the number of each type of food they brought.

Types of Food at the Picnic

Burger	Chicken	Potato Salad	Green Salad	Other
////	卌	卌 //	///	卌

Complete the table using data in the tally chart.

Type of Food	Burger		Potato Salad	Green Salad	Other
Number of Friends	4	5		3	

Complete. Use the data in the table or tally chart.

1 The most popular food was _____ .

2 What was the least popular food? _____

3 There were _____ friends at the picnic.

4 How many more friends brought potato salad than burgers for the picnic? _____

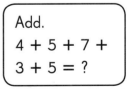

Add.
4 + 5 + 7 + 3 + 5 = ?

Subtract.
7 − 4 = ?

Guided Practice

The bar graph shows the number of different types of fruit that Raul bought at a supermarket.

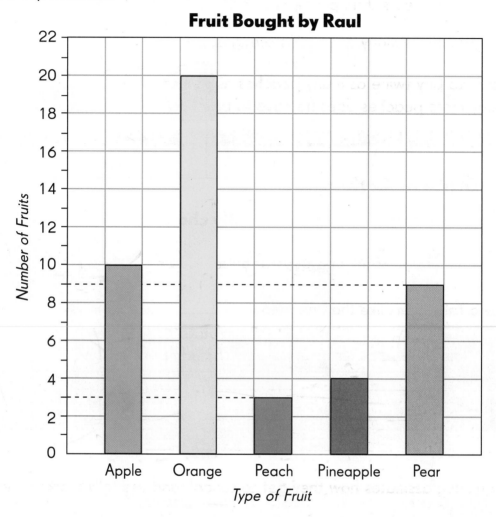

Complete the table using the data in the bar graph above.

Fruit Bought by Raul

	Type of Fruit	Number of Fruits
5	Apple	
6	Orange	
7	Peach	
8	Pineapple	
9	Pear	

Complete. Use the data in the table on page 130.

10 How many pieces of fruit did Raul buy altogether? ⬜

11 How many more pears than pineapples did Raul buy? ⬜

12 Raul bought half as many ⬜ as oranges.

13 Raul wants to buy twice as many peaches as apples.
How many more peaches does he have to buy? ⬜

 Hands-On Activity

WORKING TOGETHER Work in groups of three or four.

Materials:
- Blank tally chart
- Blank table

STEP **1** Use a tally chart like the one below.

How Students Get to School	Tally
Walk	
Bus	
Car	

STEP **2** Ask your classmates how they get to school, and use tally marks to record the data.

STEP **3** Count the tally marks and present the data in a table.

How Students Get to School	Number
Walk	
Bus	
Car	

STEP **4** Write five questions about the data in the table using these phrases.

how many students	fewer than	more than
the least	the most	altogether

Let's Practice

Study the graph. Complete the table using data in the bar graph.

The graph shows the number of passengers who used five bus routes last Monday.

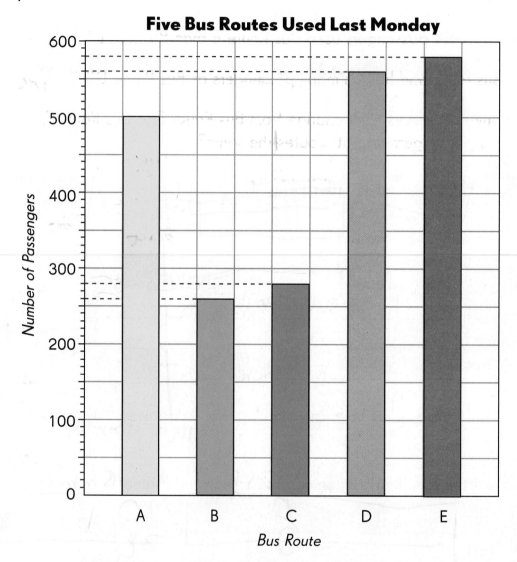

Five Bus Routes Used Last Monday

1 Five Bus Routes Used Last Monday

Bus Route	A	B	C	D	E
Number of Passengers					

Complete. Use the data in the table.

2 Which bus route was used the most? ⬜

3 Which bus route was used the least? ⬜

4 What was the total number of passengers who used the five bus routes last Monday? ⬜

5 How many more passengers used Bus Route E than Bus Route B? ⬜

6 Which bus route had half as many passengers as Bus Route D? ⬜

7 How many passengers must change from Bus Route E to Bus Route A to make the number of passengers on both routes the same? ⬜

ON YOUR OWN

Go to Workbook A:
Practice 1, pages 67–70

Lesson 4.2 Using a Table

Lesson Objective

- Read and interpret data in a table, using rows, columns, and intersections.

Vocabulary

row   intersection

column

Data in a table is organized by rows, columns, and intersections.

Mrs. Sanchez is returning home early from a business trip. Help her check the schedule to find a flight leaving for Orange County in the morning.

Step 2 Column

Flight Schedule

Destination	Departure 9:00 A.M.	Departure 2:00 P.M.	Departure 9:00 P.M.
Salt Lake City	Flight 23	Flight 24	Flight 27
Phoenix	Flight 35	Flight 67	Flight 86
Orange County	**Flight 74**	Flight 87	Flight 73
San Diego	Flight 63	Flight 26	Flight 98

Step 1 Row   **Step 3** Intersection

First, look under Destination for the row that shows Orange County.

Then, look across the column headers for a morning departure.

The intersection where the Orange County row meets the 9:00 A.M. column shows Flight 74.

Guided Practice

Study the rows, columns, and intersections. Then complete.

The number of medals won by top ranking countries in the 2006 Winter Olympics held in Turin, Italy is recorded in the table.

Medals Won by Top Ranking Countries

Country	Gold	Silver	Bronze	Total Number
Germany	11	12	6	29
United States	9	9	7	25
Austria	9	7	7	23
Russia	8	6	8	22
Canada	7	10	7	24

Source: www.abc.net.au/winterolympics/2006/fullmedal-tally.htm

1 The United States won [ ] silver medals.

2 Russia won a total of [ ] medals altogether.

3 Austria won [ ] fewer gold medals than Germany.

4 [ ], [ ], and [ ] won the same number of bronze medals.

5 The number 11 appears at the intersection of the row for [ ] and the column for [ ].

> Where does the row for the United States intersect with the column for silver medals?

Study the rows, columns, and intersections. Then complete.

A food court surveys customers to find out which type of food is most popular among three age groups of people.

Popular Types of Food

Age Group	Fast Food	Italian	Mexican	Chinese
Under 12	54	21	16	9
From 12 to 18	34	24	29	13
Over 18	11	35	26	28

6 The least number of children under the age of 12 eat [ ] food.

7 The greatest number of adults over 18 eat [ ] food.

8 The difference between the number of children under 12 who prefer Italian food to Mexican food is [   ].

9 The difference between the number of students in the 12 to 18 age group who prefer fast food to Chinese food is [   ].

10 The number of adults who prefer Mexican and Chinese food altogether is [   ].

Complete the table to answer the questions below.

Rebecca made this table to show the birthdays of her classmates in the months from January to June. All her classmates were born in the same year.
Help Rebecca complete the table.

Birthday Months of Rebecca's Classmates

Birthday Month	Number of Boys	Number of Girls	Total Number
January	2	3	5
February	4	[ ]	6
March	[ ]	2	3
April	5	[ ]	5
May	4	2	[ ]
June	[ ]	3	7
Total	[ ]	[ ]	[ ]

11 How many classmates were born in May and June? [   ]

12 How many classmates were born in these six months? [   ]

13 Which month has the greatest number of birthdays? [   ]

14 Rebecca is the youngest among those born in March.

a How many of her classmates born from January to June are older than Rebecca? [   ]

b How many of her classmates born from January to June are younger than Rebecca? [   ]

Complete the table to answer the questions below.

The table shows the number of dimes and quarters that five students collected during the first hour of a fundraising event.

Dimes and Quarters Collected at a Fundraising Event

| Student | Dimes | | Quarters | | Total Amount |
	Number of Coins Collected	Amount Collected	Number of Coins Collected	Amount Collected	
Ryan	12	$1.20	18	$4.50	$5.70
Janice	15	$	16	$	$
Steve	20	$	10	$	$
Selma	13	$	12	$	$
Ying	6	$	25	$	$
Total		$		$	$

15 Selma collected a total of $.

16 Who collected the greatest amount of money?

17 Who collected the greatest number of coins?

18 How much more did Ying collect than Janice? $

19 How much less did Steve collect than Janice? $

20 How much more must Ryan collect to match the amount that Ying has collected?
    $

 **Hands-On Activity**

Talk to your classmates to find out their favorite colors.
Record your findings. Then make a table on a computer to show the data you have collected. Present your table to the class.

Guided Practice

Complete the table to answer the questions below.

The table shows the number of bottles of water and juice sold at each booth during a fall festival.

Bottles Sold at a Fall Festival

Booth	Water (50¢ each)		Juice (80¢ each)		Total Amount
	Number of Bottles Sold	Amount Collected	Number of Bottles Sold	Amount Collected	
A	25	$12.50	20	$16.00	$28.50
B	25	$	10	$	$
C	12	$	5	$	$
D	30	$	15	$	$
Total		$		$	$

21 Which booth collected the most money?

22 Which booth collected the least money?

23 Which booths sold the greatest number of bottles of water and juice?

24 Which booth sold the least number of bottles of water and juice?

Suggest why this booth sold the least number of bottles of water and juice.

Let's Practice

Complete the table and answer the questions below.

The table shows Ms. Frey's students' favorite colors.

Favorite Colors of Ms. Frey's Students

Color	Number of Boys	Number of Girls	Total Number
Red	2	4	6
Blue		3	5
Green	3	2	
Yellow	2		4
Total		11	

1 The number 6 appears in the intersection of the row for _____ and the column for _____ .

2 The number at the intersection of the row for Green and the column for Number of Boys is _____ .

3 Which color is least popular among the students? _____

4 Which color is most popular among the girls? _____

5 How many more girls than boys like red? _____

6 Are there fewer students who like green than red? _____ If so, how many fewer? _____

7 What is the total number of boys in the class? _____

8 How many students are there in the class altogether? _____

ON YOUR OWN

Go to Workbook A: Practice 2, pages 71–74

Lesson 4.3 Line Graphs

Lesson Objectives

- Make, read, and interpret line graphs.
- Choose an appropriate graph to display a given data set.

Learn **Read a line graph to find out how data changes over time.**

The table shows the temperature at different times of the day at a school.

Temperature at a School

Time	7 A.M.	8 A.M.	9 A.M.	10 A.M.	11 A.M.	12 P.M.
Temperature (°F)	70	74	78	84	88	90

The data in the table can also be shown in this line graph.

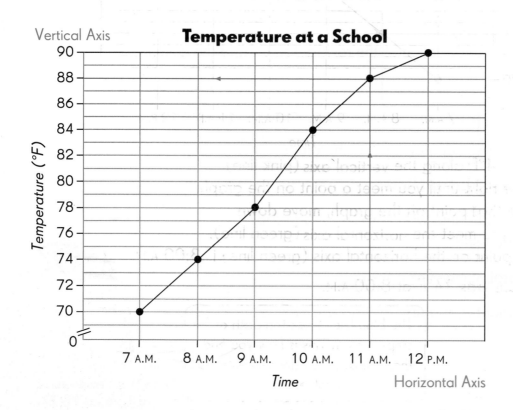

Temperature at a School

140   **Chapter 4**   Tables and Line Graphs

What is the temperature at 11:00 A.M.?

Step 1 Find 11:00 A.M. along the **horizontal axis** (green line).

Step 2 Move up until you meet a point on the graph.

Step 3 From that point on the graph, move left until you meet the **vertical axis** (pink line).

Step 4 The point on the scale, or vertical axis (pink line) is 88°F.

The temperature at 11:00 A.M. is 88°F.

At what time was the temperature 74°F.?

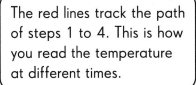

The red lines track the path of steps 1 to 4. This is how you read the temperature at different times.

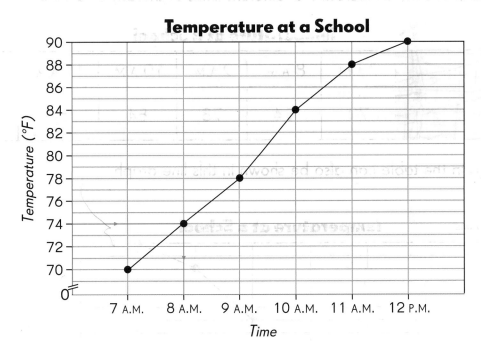

Temperature at a School

Temperature (°F) — vertical axis: 0, 70, 72, 74, 76, 78, 80, 82, 84, 86, 88, 90

Time — horizontal axis: 7 A.M., 8 A.M., 9 A.M., 10 A.M., 11 A.M., 12 P.M.

Step 1 Find 74°F along the vertical axis (pink line).

Step 2 Move right until you meet a point on the graph.

Step 3 From that point on the graph, move down until you meet the horizontal axis (green line).

Step 4 The point on the horizontal axis (green line) is 8:00 A.M.

The temperature was 74°F at 8:00 A.M.

The blue lines track the path of steps 1 to 4. This is how you find the time at which the temperature was a given value.

Guided Practice

Complete. Use the data in the line graph.

The table and line graph show the distance from Ryan's home during the first seven minutes of a bus trip.

Distance from Ryan's Home

Time after Bus Trip Begins (min)	1	2	3	4	5	6	7
Distance from Ryan's Home (m)	250	750	1,250	1,500	1,500	2,500	2,000

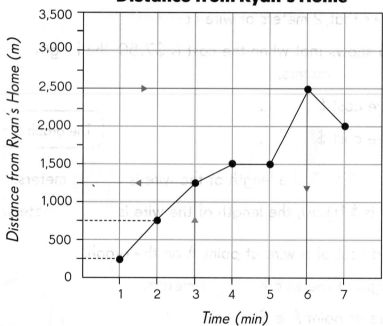

Distance from Ryan's Home

1. How far is Ryan from his home after 3 minutes on the bus?

2. After [ ] minutes on the bus, Ryan is 2,500 meters from his home.

3. The bus stopped at a bus stop between the [ ] and [ ] minute.

4. What was the increase in distance from Ryan's home from the first to the third minute?

5. After how many minutes of its journey did the bus turn around and travel in the direction of Ryan's home?

6. During which 1-minute interval was the bus moving the fastest?

Complete. Use data from the line graph.

The line graph shows the cost of a type of wire sold in a hardware store.

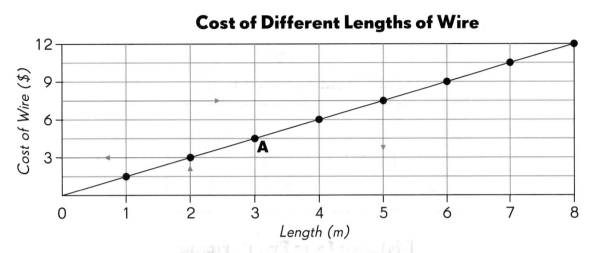

Cost of Different Lengths of Wire

7 **a** The graph shows that 2 meters of wire cost $ ____ .

b The graph also shows that when the cost is $7.50, the length
of the wire is ____ meters.

8 **a** 4 meters of wire cost $ ____ .

b 8 meters of wire cost $ ____ .

The graph is a straight line.

9 **a** When the cost is $9.00, the length of the wire is ____ meters.

b When the cost is $10.50, the length of the wire is ____ meters.

10 Find the length and cost of a wire at point A on the graph.

At point A, the length of the wire is ____ meters.

The cost of the wire at point A is $ ____ .

11 Use the graph to find the missing numbers below. What is the increase in the
cost of the wire for every 1 meter increase in length?

	1 m	1 m	1 m	1 m	Increase in length of wire
Length (m)	1	2	3	4	5
Cost ($)	1.50	3	____	____	7.50
	$1.50	____	____	____	Increase in cost of wire

For every 1 meter increase in length, the cost of the wire increases by $ ____ .

Complete. Use data from the line graph.

The line graph shows the length of a spring when various masses are hung on it.

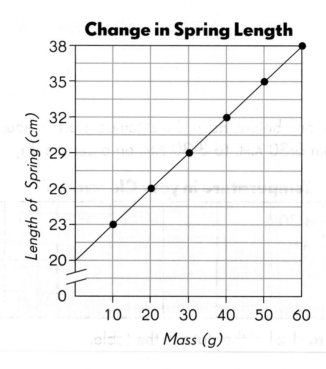

12 What is the length of the spring when it is not stretched?

13 What is the length of the spring when these masses are hung on it?

    a   10 grams

    b   30 grams

    c   40 grams

    d   50 grams

14 What is the mass hung on the spring when its length is

    a   26 centimeters?

    b   38 centimeters?

15 Compare the original length of the spring to its length when different masses are hung on it.

    a   By how many centimeters is the spring stretched when a mass of 60 grams is hung on it?

    b   If the spring is stretched by 15 centimeters, what is the mass that is hung on it?

Hands-On Activity

WORK IN PAIRS

Materials:
• Blank table
• Grid paper
• Room thermometer
• Clock

Use a table like the one below. Record the temperature in your classroom at 1-hour intervals from 8:30 A.M. to 3:30 P.M. on a certain day.

Temperature in your Classroom

Time	8:30 A.M.						3:30 P.M.
Temperature (°F)							

Make a line graph to display the data in the table.

Follow these steps to make your line graph.

STEP 1 Use grid paper.
Give the line graph a title.
Label the horizontal axis and vertical axis of the graph.

STEP 2 Choose a suitable scale on the horizontal axis to show the time.
Choose a suitable scale on the vertical axis to show the temperature.
Start with 0 and then complete the scale on both axes.

STEP 3 Plot each point on the graph and join the points.

Answer each question.

1 How did you decide on a scale for your graph?

2 What is the greatest number for your scale? Explain why.

Learn Different types of graphs show data in different ways.

Joe wrote a report on Nature Park for a class project. He used different types of graphs to show data about the park in different ways.

First, he wanted to compare the number of people who visited the park on different days of the week. He used a bar graph to show this data.

A bar graph is useful for comparing data, especially when the numbers are large.

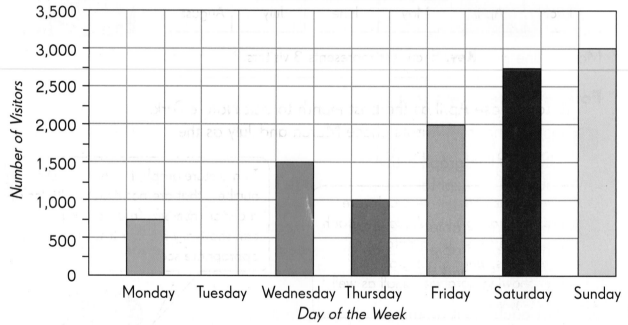

Visitors at Nature Park

There were more visitors at Nature Park on Sunday than on any other day.
On Tuesday, there were no visitors at the park.
There were 500 more visitors on Friday than on Wednesday.

We can show any number on a bar graph by choosing an appropriate scale.

Joe then surveyed 48 visitors to find out the best month to visit the park. He used a picture graph to show the results.

A picture graph is useful for showing data with numbers that are multiples of a certain number. In a picture graph, we use a key instead of a scale.

Best Month to Visit Nature Park

March	April	May	June	July	August

Key: Each ★ represents 3 visitors.

15 visitors chose April as the best month to visit Nature Park. The same number of visitors chose March and July as the best month to visit Nature Park.

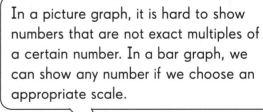

In a picture graph, it is hard to show numbers that are not exact multiples of a certain number. In a bar graph, we can show any number if we choose an appropriate scale.

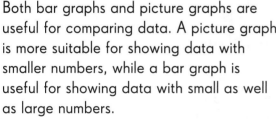

Both bar graphs and picture graphs are useful for comparing data. A picture graph is more suitable for showing data with smaller numbers, while a bar graph is useful for showing data with small as well as large numbers.

Continued on next page

Joe used a line graph to show how the temperature at the park changed over a few hours.

A line graph is useful for showing how data changes over time.

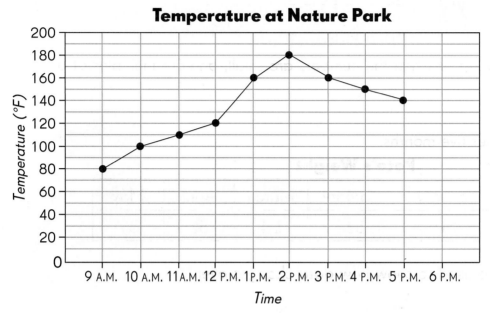

Temperature at Nature Park

The highest temperature was recorded at the park at 2:00 P.M.
The temperature at the park increased from 9:00 A.M. to 2:00 P.M., and then decreased.

Guided Practice

Choose a graph to display the data. Write bar graph, line graph, or picture graph. Explain your choice.

16 A comparison of the number of visitors to an art museum in two different months.

Visitors at an Art Museum

Month	January	February	March	April	May	June
Number of Visitors	230	80	340	630	420	540

A _____ can be used to compare data when the numbers are _____ .

17 Number of books read by some students each month.

Number of Books Read by Students

Student	Andy	Brian	Doug	Candy
Number of Books	12	8	16	4

A ⬜ can be used when the numbers are small, and are multiples of a certain number.

18 Pete's weight over five months.

Pete's Weight

Month	January	February	March	April	May
Weight (lb)	50	53	54	52	51

A ⬜ can be used to show how data changes over ⬜ .

Let's Practice

Complete. Use data from the line graph.

The line graph shows the height of a balloon above the ground between 1:00 P.M. and 6:00 P.M. on Monday.

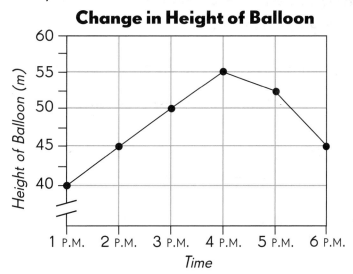

Change in Height of Balloon

1 What was the height of the balloon at **a** 1:00 P.M. ⬜   **b** 5:00 P.M.? ⬜

2 What was the greatest height the balloon reached? At what time did it reach this height?

3 In which 1-hour interval did the greatest decrease in height occur?

4 What was the difference between the greatest and lowest heights reached by the balloon?

Choose a graph to display the data. Write bar graph, line graph, or picture graph. Explain your choice.

Mrs. Tucker, the school librarian, has to make a presentation to the principal. She collected these sets of data. Can you help her select the most suitable graph for each data set?

5 Mrs. Tucker wants the principal to see the difference in the number of visitors to the library in the first few weeks of the year.

Visitors to the Library

Week	1	2	3	4	5	6
Number of Visitors	300	180	260	340	420	150

6 Mrs. Tucker asked 30 Grade 1 students their favorite choice of books so that she could plan the Young Readers' Program.

Favorite Books

Category	Adventure	Science Fiction	Mystery	Fairy Tales
Number of Students	6	3	6	15

7 Mrs. Tucker wants to show how the number of students at the library changes during the day.

Number of Students at the Library

Time	9:00 A.M.	11:00 P.M.	1:00 P.M.	3:00 P.M.
Number of students	20	28	35	12

ON YOUR OWN

**Go to Workbook A:
Practice 3, pages 75–80**

CRITICAL THINKING SKILLS
Put On Your Thinking Cap!

PROBLEM SOLVING

The tables show the number of ears of corn sold at two farm stands from Monday to Thursday last week.

Corn Sales at Farm Stand A

Day	Monday	Tuesday	Wednesday	Thursday
Number Sold	125	150	180	240

Corn Sales at Farm Stand B

Day	Monday	Tuesday	Wednesday	Thursday
Number Sold	160	235	110	185

Use the tables to answer each question.

1 How many ears of corn were sold at both stands combined on Tuesday?

2 How many ears of corn were sold at both stands combined from Monday to Thursday?

3 On which days did Stand A sell more corn than Stand B?

4 On which days did Stand A sell more than 150 ears of corn?

5 On which days did Stand B sell more than 180 ears of corn?

6 How many more ears of corn would Stand A have to sell on Tuesday in order to match the number of ears of corn sold by Stand B on the same day?

ON YOUR OWN

Go to Workbook A:
Put on Your Thinking Cap!
pages 81–82

Chapter 4 Tables and Line Graphs **151**

Chapter Wrap Up

Study Guide
You have learned...

Make and Interpret a Table

Make a table from data provided in the form of a tally chart or bar graph.

Example

Bicycle Sales

Day	Tally
Monday	卌
Tuesday	卌 /
Wednesday	卌 卌
Thursday	/
Friday	///

Bicycle Sales

Day	Bicycle Sales
Monday	5
Tuesday	6
Wednesday	10
Thursday	1
Friday	3

- On Wednesday, 4 more bicycles were sold than on Tuesday.
- Twice as many bicycles were sold on Tuesday than on Friday.

Using a Table

Data in a table is organized by rows, columns, and intersections.

Favorite Sports of a Group of Students

Sport	Number of Boys	Number of Girls	Total Number
Football	10	6	16
Basketball	12	8	20
Swimming	9	11	20

- 2 more girls than boys like swimming.
- The total number of students who like basketball is 20.

BIG IDEA
▶ Graphs and tables are visual tools for showing and analyzing data.

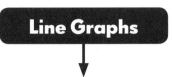

Line Graphs

↓

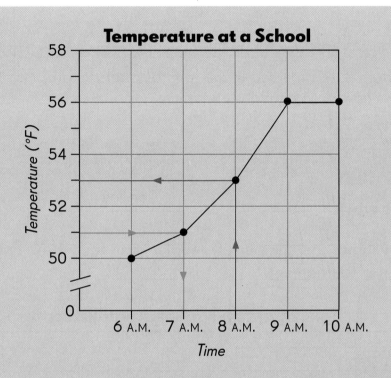

Temperature at a School

- The lowest temperature was recorded at 6:00 A.M.

- There was no change in temperature from 9:00 A.M. to 10:00 A.M.

↓

Choose an Appropriate Graph

- A bar graph is useful for comparing data, especially when the numbers are large.

- A picture graph is useful for comparing data when the numbers are small, and are multiples of a certain number.

- A line graph is used to show how data changes over time.

Chapter Review/Test

Vocabulary

Choose the correct word.

table
tally chart
row
column
intersection
horizontal axis
vertical axis
line graph

1 In a table, the place where a row and a column meet is called an _____ .

2 A _____ organizes data in groups of 5.

3 A _____ shows how data changes over time.

Concepts and Skills

Solve. Show your work.

4 The bar graph shows the number of people from each New England state participating in a tournament.

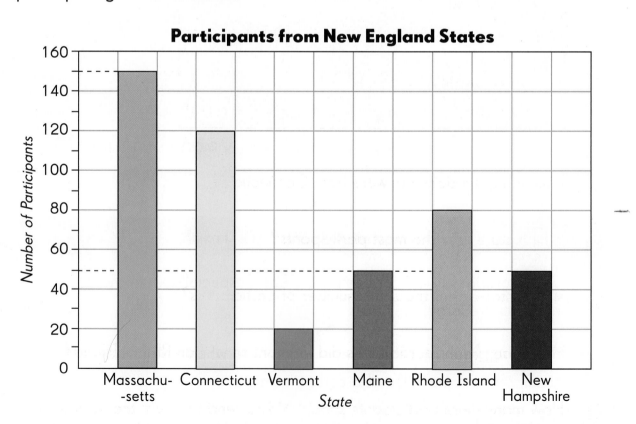

Participants from New England States

a Use the data from the bar graph to complete the table.

State	Number of Participants
Massachusetts	
Connecticut	
Vermont	
Maine	
Rhode Island	
New Hampshire	

b How many participants were from Connecticut?

c Which state sent the most participants?

d Which states sent the same number of participants?

e How many fewer participants did Vermont send than Rhode Island?

f How many more participants should Maine send to equal the number of participants from Connecticut?

5 The table shows the number of notebooks and pens bought by three classes in a school.

Stationery Bought by Three Classes

| Class | Notebooks ($2 each) | | Pens (80¢ each) | | Total Cost |
	Number of Notebooks Bought	Cost	Number of Pens Bought	Cost	
A	12	$	6	$	$
B	15	$		$8.00	$
C		$16.00	8	$	$
Total		$		$	$

a Which class bought the most pens and notebooks altogether? [ ]

b Which class spent the least amount of money on stationery? [ ]

c What is the total cost of pens bought by the three classes? [ ]

d Class A spent more money on [ ] than on [ ] .

How much more was it? [ ]

6 The line graph shows the amount of gas left in a car's tank and the distance the car traveled.

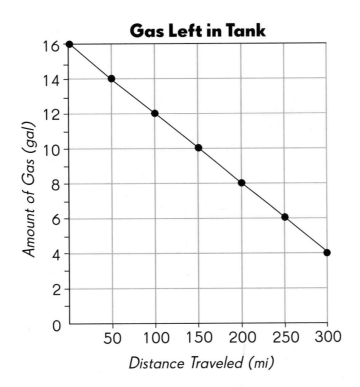

Gas Left in Tank

a How much gas was in the car's tank at

   i the start of the trip?

   ii the end of the trip?

b How much gas was used for

   i the first 50 miles traveled?

   ii the second 50 miles traveled?

   iii the third 50 miles traveled?

   iv the fourth 50 miles traveled?

c Look at your answers in Exercise 6b.

   i How far can this car travel on 2 gallons of gas?

   ii How far can it travel on 1 gallon of gas?

7 The line graph shows the number of people in line at a post office from 9:00 A.M. to 3:00 P.M.

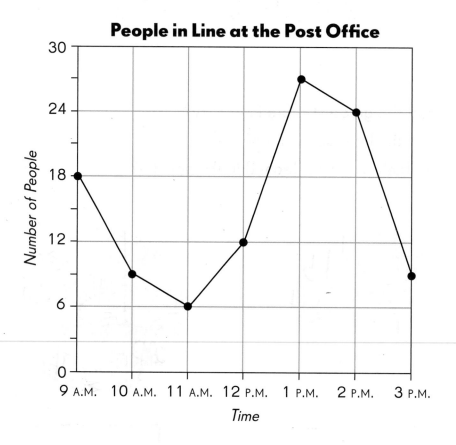

People in Line at the Post Office

Number of People

Time

a At what time was the line the shortest?

b At what time was the line the longest?

c **i** What was the decrease in the number of people in the line from 10:00 A.M. to 11:00 A.M.?

ii In which 1-hour interval did the line decrease by the same number of people as from 10:00 A.M. to 11:00 A.M.?

d What would be the best time to use this post office? State a reason for your answer.

5 Data and Probability

Which team had the greatest score in one try?

Which team had the least score in one try?

What is a more likely score for Team B in the next try?

Team A

1st try: *50 points*
2nd try: *8 points*
3rd try: *8 points*

Team B

1st try: *17 points*
2nd try: *28 points*
3rd try: *24 points*

BIG IDEAS

► Information can be analyzed to find a typical value for a data set.
► Data can be analyzed to predict the likelihood of an event happening.

Interpreting data in a tally chart

The tally chart shows the number of art shows in the months January through June.

Number of Art Shows

Month	Number of Art Shows
January	ⅲⅲ │
February	ⅲⅲ ‖
March	‖│
April	ⅲⅲ ‖
May	ⅲⅲ
June	ⅲⅲ ⅲⅲ ‖

The greatest number of art shows were held in June.
The same number of art shows were held in February and April.
The total number of art shows held in this survey is 40.

Interpreting data in a table

The table shows the number of points scored by each player.

Points Scored

Player	Number of Points
Alex	12
Tony	25
Kayla	9
Jane	18
Tyler	30

Tony scored 25 points.
Jane scored twice as many points as Kayla.
Tyler scored 18 points more than Alex.
Kayla needs to score 21 more points in order to match Tyler.

Interpreting data in a line plot

The line plot shows the number of pets owned by a class of students.
Each X represents 1 student.

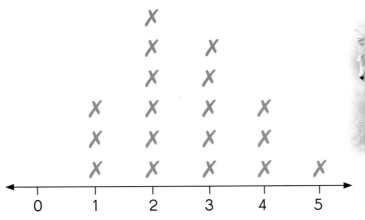

Number of Pets

Five students own 3 pets each.
The most common number of pets is 2.
The number of students who own 1 pet and 4 pets is the same.
The total number of students in the class is 18.
Four students own more than 3 pets.

Showing parts of a whole or divisions on a number line

The number line shows some fraction values from 0 to 1.

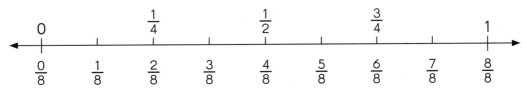

The number line is divided into 8 equal parts.

$\frac{3}{4}$ and $\frac{7}{8}$ are greater than $\frac{1}{2}$.

$\frac{1}{4}$ and $\frac{1}{8}$ are closer to 0 than to 1.

$\frac{1}{4}$ and $\frac{2}{8}$ are equivalent fractions.

Quick Check

Use the data in the tally chart to complete the table.

The tally chart shows the sports that a class of students plays.

Sports Played by a Class

Sport	Number of Students
Basketball	~~IIII~~ III
Baseball	~~IIII~~ I
Football	IIII
Swimming	IIII
Tennis	II

Sports Played by a Class

Sport	Number of Students
Basketball	8
Baseball	
Football	
Swimming	
Tennis	

Complete. Use the data in the table.

1 The greatest number of students play [   ].

2 There are [   ] students in the class.

3 [   ] more students play basketball than tennis.

4 The same number of students go for [   ] and [   ].

5 Four times as many students play [   ] as tennis.

6 [   ] more students must take up swimming to match the number of students who play basketball.

Complete. Use the data in the line plot.

The line plot shows the number of games won by different people at a carnival.
Each ✗ represents one person.

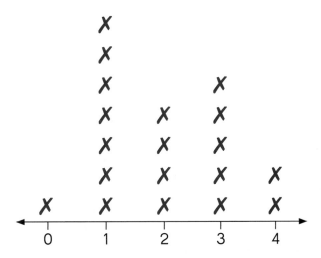

Number of Games Won

7 How many people won 4 games each?

8 How many people won more than 1 game?

9 The highest number of games won is   .

10   as many people won 2 games as the number of people
who won 4 games.

11   people won fewer than 2 games.

12 The least number of games won is   .

13 How many people were there in all?

Use the number line to complete the data.

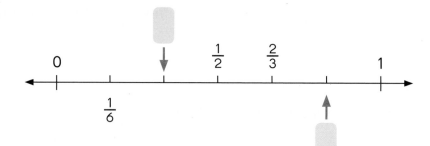

14. The number line has [   ] equal parts.

15. Each part is equal to [ ]/[ ].

16. The missing fractions are [ ]/[ ] and [ ]/[ ].

Use greater than or closer to to complete the sentences.

17. $\frac{2}{3}$ is [   ] $\frac{1}{2}$.

18. $\frac{1}{6}$ is [   ] 0 than to 1.

19. $\frac{2}{3}$ is [   ] 1 than to 0.

20. $\frac{1}{2}$ is [   ] $\frac{1}{6}$.

 **Average**

Lesson Objective

• Describe a data set using the average or mean.

Vocabulary

average

mean

Learn **Divide to find the** 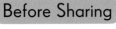**.**

Andrew has 4 shells, Beth has 9 shells, and Cynthia has 8 shells. If all the shells are shared equally among the children, how many shells would each child get?

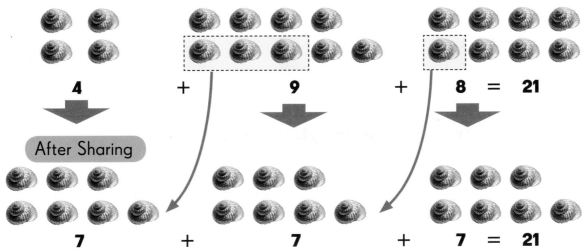

Before Sharing

4 + 9 + 8 = 21

After Sharing

7 + 7 + 7 = 21

Step 1 Find the total number of shells.
4 + 9 + 8 = 21 shells

Step 2 Divide the total number of shells by the number of children.
21 ÷ 3 = 7 shells
Each child gets 7 shells.

21 ÷ 3 can also be written as $\frac{21}{3}$.

Average number of shells for each child $= \dfrac{\text{Total number of shells}}{\text{Number of children}}$

The number of shells that each child will get if they are shared equally is 7.
The average of 4, 9, and 8 is 7.

Hands-On Activity

Materials:
- Connecting cubes

Work in groups of four.
Use the set of data that your teacher gives you. Pairs in each group work together to find the average of the data by using two methods.

Example **2, 5, 8**

Method 1
Find the average by evening out the numbers in the data.

STEP 1 Use connecting cubes and stack them to show each number.

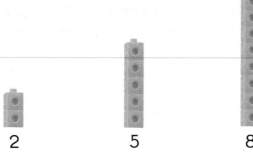

STEP 2 Move the connecting cubes around until each stack has the same number of connecting cubes.

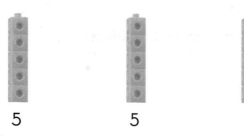

The average of the numbers is 5.

> Average is a number used to describe how the whole set of data is divided up so that each part gets the same amount.

Method 2
Find the average by using the formula.

$$\text{Average} = \frac{\text{Total number or amount}}{\text{Number of items}}$$

$$= \frac{2 + 5 + 8}{3} = 5$$

Guided Practice

Find the average.

1 Four students sold stickers for charity. The table shows the number of stickers each student sold.

Number of Stickers Sold for Charity

Name	Number of Stickers
Abe	12
Bette	20
Carlo	16
Diana	28

What is the average number of stickers that each student sold?

Average number of stickers sold by each student = $\dfrac{\text{Total number of stickers sold}}{\text{Number of students}}$

Total = 12 + ____ + ____ + ____ = ____

Average = ____ ÷ ____ = ____

The average number of stickers that each student sold is ____ .

Learn **Another word for average is mean.**

These are the scores Lila, Jody, and Chris got on an English test.

Mean or average = $\dfrac{\text{Total number or amount}}{\text{Number of items}}$

Continued on next page

What is the total of the 3 scores?

Total score = 78 + 84 + 75
            = 237

The total score that Lila, Jody, and Chris got is 237.

What is their mean score?

Mean score = 237 ÷ 3
           = 79

Their mean score is 79.

For data sets that do not have very high or very low numbers, the mean or average gives a good description of the data.

Guided Practice

Find the mean or average.

A farmer has 5 dogs whose weights are 28 pounds, 34 pounds, 56 pounds, 42 pounds, and 60 pounds.

2 What is the total weight of the 5 dogs?

Total weight = [ ] + [ ] + [ ] + [ ] + [ ]
             = [ ] lb

The total weight of the 5 dogs is [ ] pounds.

3 What is the mean weight of the 5 dogs?

Mean weight = [ ] ÷ [ ]
            = [ ] lb

The mean weight of the 5 dogs is [ ] pounds.

Learn — Find the total from the mean or average.

Gina had 4 tests last week. Her mean score for the 4 tests was 82. What was her total score for the 4 tests?

Mean score for the 4 tests = 82

Number of tests she took = 4

Total score for the 4 tests = 82 × 4
                             = 328

Her total score for the 4 tests was 328.

> Total score
> = Score for each test × Number of tests
> Since the score for each test is different, use the mean score.
> Total score
> = Mean score × Number of tests

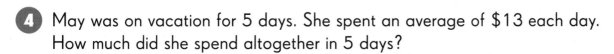

Total number or amount
= Mean or average × Number of items

Guided Practice

Find the total from the mean or average.

4 May was on vacation for 5 days. She spent an average of $13 each day. How much did she spend altogether in 5 days?

Average amount of money spent each day = $ ☐

Number of days = ☐

Total amount spent = $ ☐ × ☐
                    = $ ☐

The total amount May spent in 5 days was $ ☐ .

Hands-On Activity

WORKING TOGETHER

Materials:
- Measuring tape
- Blank table

Work in groups of six.

Use a measuring tape to measure the length of each group member's arm and his/her height to the nearest inch. Record your answers in a table and answer the questions below.

Arm Length and Height of Group Members

Name	Arm Length (in.)	Height (in.)

1 Who has the longest arm?

2 Who has the shortest arm?

3 The average arm length of the group is _____ inches.

4 The average height of the group is _____ inches.

5 Is it true that the tallest person has the longest arm?

Let's Explore!

WORKING TOGETHER

Materials:
• 3 strips of ribbon, each 30 cm long

Work in groups of three.

Use 3 strips of ribbon, A, B, and C, each with a length of 30 centimeters.

STEP 1 Cut Ribbon A into 5 pieces of different lengths. Measure the lengths of the 5 pieces, then find their mean length.

STEP 2 Repeat **STEP 1** for Ribbon B, but cut it into 5 pieces with lengths different from those above. Then find their mean length.

STEP 3 Cut Ribbon C into 5 equal pieces. Find their mean length.
Compare the mean lengths in each step above.
Are they different? Discuss your answer.

Math Journal

Study the number sentences and pictures. Then write a word problem based on each set of number sentence and picture.

1 $300 \div 4 = 75$

2 $72 \times 3 = 216$

3 **a** $16 + 12 + 20 = 48$ **b** $48 \div 3 = 16$

$16 $12 $20

Let's Practice

Find the average or mean of each data set.

1 4, 6, 10, 12, 18

2 4, 8, 10, 13, 16, 21

3 $4, $8, $5, $28, $35

4 12 L, 26 L, 18 L, 27 L, 42 L

5 38 m, 46 m, 72 m, 84 m

Complete. Use the data in the table.

The number of points that Mark scored in 5 basketball games is shown in the table.

Points Scored by Mark

Game	First	Second	Third	Fourth	Fifth
Number of Points	12	8	6	4	0

6 What was the total number of points for the 5 games Mark played?

7 What was Mark's mean number of points for the 5 games?

Solve. Show your work.

8 Maria bought 18 rolls of ribbon. The average length of each roll of ribbon is 6 feet. Find the total length of all the rolls of ribbon.

9 In 4 games, a basketball team scored a total of 224 points. What was the team's average score in the 4 games?

10 The total weight of 18 bricks is 54 pounds. Find the average weight of the bricks.

11 Simon is filling 13 pitchers with cranberry juice. There is an average of 975 milliliters of cranberry juice in each pitcher. What is the total volume of cranberry juice in the 13 pitchers altogether? Give your answer in liters and milliliters.

ON YOUR OWN

Go to Workbook A: Practice 1, pages 93–100

Lesson 5.2 Median, Mode, and Range

Lesson Objectives

- Find the mean, median, mode, and range of a set of data.
- Make and interpret line plots.

Learn **Find the median of a data set.**

Paul picked 5 numbers from a bag. He ordered them from least to greatest.

7	9	14	18	26
least				greatest

The middle number, or the median, is 14.

> When a set of data having one middle number is arranged from least to greatest, the middle number is the median.

Paul then picked another number, 21, from the bag. He arranged the numbers in order again.

7	9	14	18	21	26
least					greatest

The numbers 14 and 18 are the middle numbers. To find the median, find the mean of the two middle numbers.

$$\text{Mean} = \frac{14 + 18}{2} = \frac{32}{2} = 16$$

The median is 16.

> When a set of data having two middle numbers is arranged from least to greatest, the median is the mean of the two middle numbers.

For data sets that have some numbers much higher or lower than most other numbers, the median gives a better description of the data than the mean.

Guided Practice

Find the median of each set of data.

Each data set shows the heights of a group of students.

1 127 cm 130 cm 140 cm 137 cm 135 cm 148 cm 150 cm

Ordered from least to greatest:

The median is ____ centimeters.

2 120 cm 145 cm 156 cm 174 cm 156 cm 135 cm 167 cm

The median is ____ centimeters.

3 118 cm 143 cm 172 cm 126 cm

158 cm 161 cm 137 cm 153 cm

The two middle numbers are ____ and ____ .

The mean of the two numbers is $\dfrac{\boxed{} + \boxed{}}{2} = \boxed{}$.

The median is ____ centimeters.

4 132 cm 143 cm 108 cm 126 cm

143 cm 175 cm 139 cm 156 cm

The median is ____ centimeters.

 **Hands-On Activity**

WORKING TOGETHER

Work in groups of four.

Use the set of data that your teacher gives you. Pairs in each group work together to find the median of the data by using two methods.

Example   The data shows the number of prizes won by a group of students.

1, 1, 2, 2, 2, 3, 4, 4, 4, 4, 5, 5, 6, 6, 6

Method 1

Find the median by marking off pairs of data starting at each end.

X, X, 2, 2, 2, 3, 4, 4, 4, 4, 5, 5, 6, 6, 6

The number that remains after marking off pairs of data is the middle number. So, the median is 4.

Method 2

Find the median of the data set using a **line plot** .

STEP 1 Draw a line plot to show the given data. Each X should represent one student.

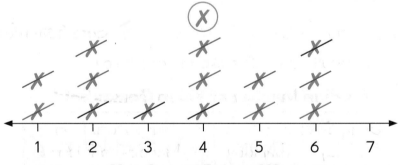

Number of Prizes Won

STEP 2 Mark off pairs of Xs starting at the ends from the bottom up. The X above the number 4 that remains after marking off the pairs is the middle number. So, the median is 4.

A line plot uses a number line to show the number of times an item of data occurs.

Let's Explore!

The table shows the number of video games a shop sold on 5 days of the week.

Number of Video Games Sold

Day	Monday	Tuesday	Wednesday	Thursday	Friday
Number of Video Games Sold	215	279	312	198	1,211

STEP 1 Find the mean using

a data only from Monday to Thursday.   **b** data from Monday to Friday.

Record your results in a table like the one below.

Mean Number of Video Games Sold

	Using Data only from Monday to Thursday	Using Data from Monday to Friday
Mean		

STEP 2 Find the median using

a data only from Monday to Thursday.   **b** data from Monday to Friday.

Record your results in a table like the one below.

Median Number of Video Games Sold

	Using Data only from Monday to Thursday	Using Data from Monday to Friday
Median		

STEP 3 Look at the two tables showing the mean and median number of video games sold. Is the mean or median more typical of this set of data? Why? Why do you think many more video games were sold on Friday than on any other day?

Find the mode of a data set.

Paul conducted a survey to find out the number of hours his classmates spend on homework each day. He recorded his data like this.

Number of Hours Spent on Homework

Number of Hours	Tally	Number of Classmates
1	//	2
2	##//	5
3	//	2
4	/	1

Paul made a line plot to show the same data.

Each ✗ represents one classmate.

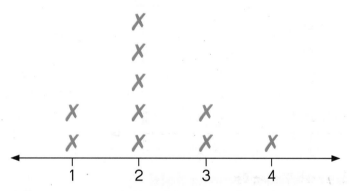

Number of Hours Spent on Homework

The number 4 has the least number of ✗s.
So, the least number of classmates
spend 4 hours on homework each day.

The number 2 has the greatest number of ✗s.
So, the greatest number of classmates
spend 2 hours on homework each day.
So, the mode of this set of data is 2.

> The mode is the number that occurs most often.

For a data set that has many identical numbers, the mode may give the best description of the data.

A set of data can have more than 1 mode. If all the numbers in a set of data appear the same number of times, there is no mode.

Guided Practice

Complete. Use data in the line plot.

Hillary counted the number of pencils each of her 18 classmates had. She made a line plot to show the data she collected. Each **X** represents 1 classmate.

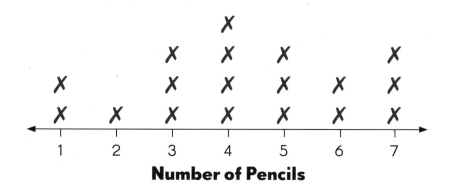

Number of Pencils

5 [ ] classmates had 1 pencil each.

6 [ ] classmates had the greatest number of pencils.

7 The mode of this set of data is [ ].

8 A new student joined Hillary's class. She had 7 pencils.

a Add an **X** to the line plot above to show this information.

b Does this change the mode of the set of data? What are the modes of the set of data now? [ ]

Let's Explore!

WORKING TOGETHER

Materials:
- Number cards
- Blank line plots

Work in groups of three.

STEP 1 Use a set of cards numbered from 1 to 6. Shuffle the cards, and place them face down.

STEP 2 Take turns to draw a card and record the number on a line plot. Cards should be replaced at the end of each turn.

STEP 3 Play 20 rounds. Then compare the three line plots. What is the mode of each player's set of data? What is the median? Describe any pattern you see.

Learn **Find the range of a data set.**

Look at Paul's line plot again. It shows the number of hours his classmates spend on homework each day.

Number of Hours Spent on Homework

The least number of hours is 1, and the greatest number of hours is 4.
The difference between these numbers is $4 - 1 = 3$.
The range of this set of numbers is 3.

> The difference between the least number and the greatest number is the range.
> Range = Greatest number − Least number

A line plot shows data arranged on a number line. It is useful for identifying the mode, median, and range.

Guided Practice

Complete. Use the data in the line plot.

Jared took a survey to see how many computer games his classmates have. His results are shown in the line plot. Each X represents one classmate.

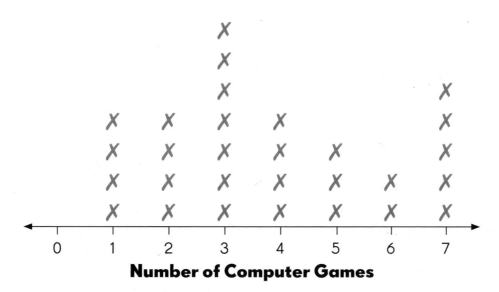

Number of Computer Games

9 The greatest number of computer games Jared's classmates have is ⬚.

10 The least number of computer games his classmates have is ⬚.

11 The range of the set of data is ⬚ − ⬚ = ⬚.

Learn **Find the mean of a data set using a line plot.**

Mrs. Curtis' class went on a trip to a fruit farm. The students picked ripe fruit from the trees. The line plot shows the number of pieces of ripe fruit that each student picked.

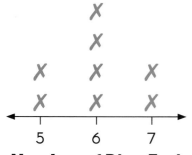

Number of Ripe Fruit

Continued on next page

To find the mean, first calculate the total number of pieces of ripe fruit the students picked.

2 students picked 5 pieces each $\longrightarrow$ 2 × 5 = 10
4 students picked 6 pieces each $\longrightarrow$ 4 × 6 = 24
2 students picked 7 pieces each $\longrightarrow$ 2 × 7 = 14

Mean = $\dfrac{\text{Total number of pieces of ripe fruit picked}}{\text{Total number of students}}$

= $\dfrac{10 + 24 + 14}{2 + 4 + 2}$ = $\dfrac{48}{8}$ = 6

The mean number of ripe fruit picked is 6.

Guided Practice

Complete. Use the data in the line plot.

The line plot shows the number of flowers each geranium plant had over a month. Each **X** represents one geranium plant.

```
   X           X
   X           X
   X           X
   X     X     X
 ──┼─────┼─────┼──→
   6     7     8
```
Number of Flowers

12 ⬜ plants had 6 flowers each. $\longrightarrow$ ⬜ × ⬜ = ⬜

13 ⬜ plant had 7 flowers. $\longrightarrow$ ⬜ × ⬜ = ⬜

14 ⬜ plants had 8 flowers each. $\longrightarrow$ ⬜ × ⬜ = ⬜

15 There were ⬜ flowers altogether.

16 There were ⬜ plants altogether.

17 The mean number of flowers each geranium plant had was ⬜.
Can you predict the mean just by looking at the data?

Math Journal

The set of numbers is arranged in order.

2, 4, 6, 12, 12, 18, 20, 32

Are the statements below true or false? If the statement is false, explain how to change the numbers or words to make it true.

1 The mode of the data set is 12 because it appears twice.

2 There is no median for this set of data because the set of numbers is even and there is no middle number.

3 The mean and median of this set of data are the same.

Let's Practice

Find the median.

The table shows the temperature at noon from Monday to Saturday.

Temperature in Fahrenheit (°F)

	Monday	Tuesday	Wednesday	Thursday	Friday	Saturday
Week 1	39°	47°	39°	52°	28°	55°
Week 2	32°	66°	47°	54°	68°	48°

1 The median temperature in Week 1 is ____ °F.

2 The median temperature in Week 2 is ____ °F.

Complete. Use the data in the line plot.

The line plot shows the number of players who scored 2, 3, or 4 goals
in their matches.
Each X represents one player.

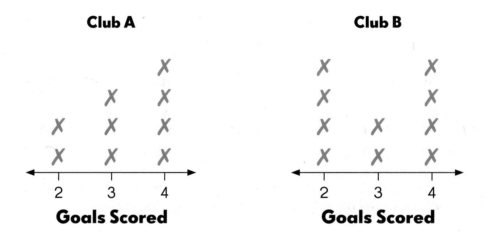

Club A

Club B

3 How many players were goal scorers in each club? ▢

4 What is the median number of goals scored by the players in

ⓐ Club A? ▢   **ⓑ** Club B? ▢

Complete. Use the data in the line plot.

Mr. Gupta sells fabric. The line plot shows the lengths of fabric
his customers bought in one afternoon.

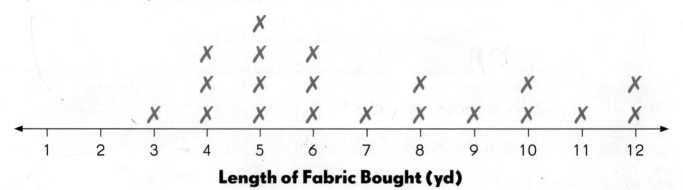

Length of Fabric Bought (yd)

5 What is the range of the lengths of fabric bought? ▢

6 What is the mode of the set of data? Is the mode typical of this set of data?

▢

7 What is the median of the set of data? Is the median typical of this set of data?

8 What is the mean of this set of data? Is the mean typical of this set of data?

9 **ⓐ** At the end of the day, another customer buys 196 yards of fabric. What is the mean, median, and mode of the new data set?

ⓑ Do the new mean, median, and mode seem typical of the data set?

Make a line plot to show the data. Use your line plot to answer each question.

A group of children went fishing at a neighborhood creek. They counted and weighed the fish they caught. The tally chart shows this data.

Number of Fish Caught

Weight of Fish (lb)	Tally	Number
1	///	3
2	//// /	6
3	////	4
4	/	1
5	/	1

10 How many fish were caught altogether?

11 What is the range of the weight of fish caught?

12 What is the mode of the set of data?

13 What is the median of the set of data?

Complete. Use the data in the line plot.

Members of a running club recorded the number of marathons they ran in a line plot.

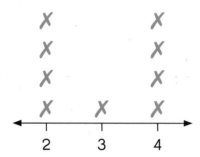

Number of Marathons Run

14 What is the total number of marathons the club members have run altogether?

15 Can you find the mean without calculating? Why?

Use the table to find each median.

Dakota counted the number of falling meteors in the sky during the August meteor showers for three years.

August Meteor Showers for Three Years

	Day 1	Day 2	Day 3	Day 4	Day 5	Day 6
Year 1	45	43	31	38	49	53
Year 2	55	40	45	49	51	58
Year 3	42	39	36	34	35	36

16 The median number of meteors in Year 1 is   .

17 The median number of meteors in Year 2 is   .

18 The median number of meteors in Year 3 is   .

19 The greatest median number of meteors was recorded in Year   .

20 The difference between the greatest and the least median number of meteors is   .

21 The median number of meteors recorded on Day 5 is   .

ON YOUR OWN

Go to Workbook A:
Practice 2, pages 101–108

Lesson 5.3 Stem-and-Leaf Plots

Lesson Objectives

- Organize and represent data in a stem-and-leaf plot.
- Use a stem-and-leaf plot to find median, mode, and range.

Vocabulary
stem-and-leaf plot
outlier

Learn Make a stem-and-leaf plot.

These are the grades that ten students scored on a math assignment.

(71) (58) (56) (69) (42) (72) (64) (56) (44) (88)

Make a stem-and-leaf-plot to organize the data.

Step 1
Order the grades from least to greatest.

(42) (44) (56) (56) (58) (64) (69) (71) (72) (88)

Step 2
Put the digits in the tens place in the 'stem' column.

Math Assignment Grades	
Stem	**Leaves**
4	2 4
5	6 6 8
6	4 9
7	1 2
8	8

4 | 2 = 42

Step 3
Put the digits in the ones place in the 'leaves' column.

The data ranges from 42 to 88, so list the tens 4 through 8 as stems.

For the grades 42 and 44, the numbers in the ones place are 2 and 4. Write 2 and 4 side by side in the leaves column to represent the ones place for both 42 and 44. Order the numbers in the 'leaves' column from least to greatest.

Use a stem-and-leaf plot to find median, mode, and range.

A stem-and-leaf plot shows data organized by place value. The leaves are the ones digits. The stems are the digits to the left of the ones digits.

Use the stem-and-leaf plot on page 187.

1 Find the median.

Count the leaves. Since there are 10 leaves, the set of data has two middle numbers — 58 and 64. The mean of 58 and 64 is the median.

$$\text{Median} = \frac{58 + 64}{2} = \frac{122}{2} = 61$$

2 Find the mode.

The grade that occurs the greatest number of times is 56.

$\boxed{42}$ $\boxed{44}$ $\boxed{56}$ $\boxed{56}$ $\boxed{58}$ $\boxed{64}$ $\boxed{69}$ $\boxed{71}$ $\boxed{72}$ $\boxed{88}$

The mode is 56.

3 Find the range.

The least number is the first number in the first row of the stem-and-leaf plot, and the greatest number is the last number in the last row.

$$\text{Range} = 88 - 42$$
$$= 46$$

An **outlier** is any number in the data that is much farther away from the largest group of data. The outlier in this set of data is 88.

A stem-and-leaf plot is useful for finding median, mode, and range.

It is easier to find the mean directly from the set of data than from a stem-and leaf plot.

Guided Practice

Complete. Use the data in the stem-and-leaf plot.

The stem-and-leaf plot shows the weights of some crates of potatoes at a supermarket.

Weight of Crates (lb)	
Stem	Leaves
2	5
3	0 4 4 7
4	8
5	2 8
6	9

2 | 5 = 25

1 For the number 58, 5 is in the _____ column, and 8 is in the _____ column.

2 The stem 3 has _____ leaves.

3 The weight that appears most often is _____ pounds. The mode is _____ pounds.

4 The median of the set of data is _____ pounds.

5 The greatest weight of a crate of potatoes is _____ pounds.

6 The least weight of a crate of potatoes is _____ pounds.

7 The difference between the least and the greatest weight of a crate of potatoes is _____ pounds. The range of the set of data is _____ pounds.

8 The total weight of all the crates of potatoes is _____ pounds.

 **Hands-On Activity**

Tech Connection

Use the internet to find the scores of each player on your favorite basketball team in a recent game. Make a stem-and-leaf plot to show the scores. Then find the median, mode, and range. Does your set of data have an outlier?

Let's Practice

Make stem-and-leaf plots to show each set of data.
Then complete the sentences.

The table shows the masses of baby elephants born in two zoos in a year.

Masses of Baby Elephants Born in Two Zoos

Zoo A	56 kg	62 kg	88 kg	96 kg	78 kg	76 kg	62 kg
Zoo B	74 kg	65 kg	65 kg	52 kg	65 kg	93 kg	

1 The mode of the masses of baby elephants born in Zoo B is _____ kilograms.

2 The mode of the masses of baby elephants born in Zoo _____ is less than the mode of the masses of those born in Zoo _____.

3 The median mass of baby elephants born in Zoo B is _____ kilograms.

4 The range of the masses of baby elephants born in Zoo A is _____ kilograms.

5 The total mass of baby elephants born in Zoo _____ is greater than the total mass of those born in Zoo _____.

The table shows the number of crafts a group of students made for a fair.

Number of Crafts Made

Student	Number of Crafts
Rachel	51
Cheyenne	44
Stella	64
Alisha	38
Michelle	44
Jordan	32
Andrew	47
Jen	40

6 The range of the set of data is _____ .

7 The mode of the set of data is _____ .

8 The median of the set of data is _____ .

9 There are _____ leaves for the place value of 3 tens.

10 There are _____ leaves for the place value of 4 tens.

ON YOUR OWN

Go to Workbook A:
Practice 3, pages 109–112

Lesson 5.4 Outcomes

Lesson Objective

- Decide whether an outcome is certain, more likely, equally likely, less likely, or impossible.

Learn Use data to predict if a result is more likely or less likely .

A bag contains 7 blue marbles and 2 yellow marbles.

When a marble is drawn from the bag, the result is called an **outcome** .
If a blue marble is drawn, the outcome is a blue marble. If a yellow marble is drawn, the outcome is a yellow marble.

Only a blue or a yellow marble can be drawn from the bag. So there are only two possible outcomes.

Since there are more blue marbles than yellow marbles, you are **more likely** to pick a blue marble than a yellow marble.

Because there are only two yellow marbles, you are **less likely** to pick a yellow marble.

Use data to predict if a result is certain or impossible.

2 yellow marbles are removed from the bag.

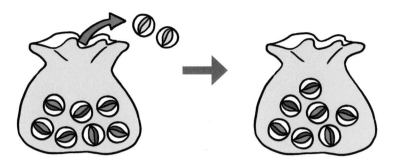

Since there are only blue marbles left in the bag, it is **certain** that a blue marble will be drawn.

Since there are no yellow marbles left in the bag, it is **impossible** to pick a yellow marble.

Use data to predict if two results are equally likely to occur.

The bag contains 5 blue marbles and 5 yellow marbles.

The number of blue marbles is the same as the number of yellow marbles.

Since there are an equal number of blue and yellow marbles, it is **equally likely** that the outcome will be a blue marble or a yellow marble.

Learn **Predict the likelihood of an outcome.**

Each spinner is spun once. Find the possible outcomes for each spinner, and the likelihood of landing on blue.

Possible Outcomes	Blue	Blue, Yellow	Blue, Purple	Yellow, Purple
Likelihood of Landing on Blue	Certain	Equally likely	Less likely	Impossible

Guided Practice

Describe the likelihood of each outcome as more likely, less likely, equally likely, certain, or impossible.

1 Look at the bags of cubes. A cube is drawn from each bag.

Possible Outcomes	Green	Green, Yellow	Green, Yellow	Green, Yellow	Yellow
Likelihood of Picking a Green Cube					

Find the possible outcomes. Then describe the likelihood of each outcome as more likely, less likely, equally likely, certain, or impossible.

2   Look at the spinners. Each spinner is spun once.

Possible Outcomes				
Likelihood of Landing on Blue				

Let's Explore!

Materials:
• Blank spinners

WORKING TOGETHER

Work in groups of three.

Each group is given blank spinners. Design your own spinners by dividing the circles into 4, 6, or 8 equal parts and coloring each part. Show and record the possible outcomes when each spinner is spun once.

Describe the likelihood of each outcome as

1 Impossible

2 Certain

3 More likely

4 Less likely

5 Equally likely

  **Hands-On Activity**

Materials:
- Connecting cubes
- Blank table
- Blank tally chart

You and your partner are given a bag with 10 red, 5 yellow, and 15 blue connecting cubes.

STEP 1 Take turns to draw a connecting cube from the bag 20 times, replacing the connecting cube each time.

STEP 2 Record your results in a table like the one below.

Color of Connecting Cube	Number
Red	
Yellow	
Blue	

STEP 3 Use a tally chart like the one below to display the same data.

Color of Connecting Cube	Tally
Red	
Yellow	
Blue	

Let's Practice

Which of the following is a possible outcome?

1 It will rain today.

2 The head appears when you toss a coin.

3 The numbers 3 and 6 appear at the same time when you throw a number cube with numbers 1, 2, 3, 4, 5, and 6.

4 A fish walks on two legs.

Draw six colored marbles in each bag to match each likelihood.

5

Bag	Bag 1	Bag 2
Likelihood of Picking a Red Marble	Certain	Impossible

6

Bag	Bag 3	Bag 4	Bag 5
Likelihood of Picking a Red Marble	More likely	Less likely	Equally likely

ON YOUR OWN

Go to Workbook A: Practice 4, pages 113–114

5.5 Probability as a Fraction

Lesson Objectives

- Determine the probability of an event.
- Express probability as a fraction.

Learn **Express the likelihood of an outcome as a fraction.**

The spinner has 6 equal parts. When the spinner is spun once, there are 6 possible outcomes. The likelihood of landing on any 1 of the 6 outcomes is equal. So, the chance of getting any 1 of the numbers is 1 out of 6, or $\frac{1}{6}$.

A **favorable outcome** is a result you are looking for.
If you are hoping to land on 5, then 5 is the favorable outcome.

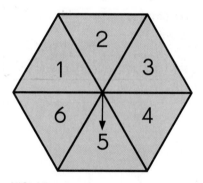

The likelihood or **probability** of getting a favorable outcome can be written as a fraction.

$$\text{Probability of a favorable outcome} = \frac{\text{Number of favorable outcomes}}{\text{Total number of possible outcomes}}$$

Likelihood or probability of landing on $5 = \frac{1}{6}$

Joe wants to land on a number less than 4.
His favorable outcomes are 1, 2, and 3.

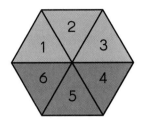

There are 3 favorable outcomes out of 6 possible outcomes.

Probability of landing
on a number less than 4 $= \dfrac{\text{Number of favorable outcomes}}{\text{Number of possible outcomes}}$

$$= \dfrac{3}{6} = \dfrac{1}{2}$$

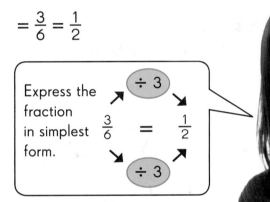

Express the fraction in simplest form.

$$\dfrac{3}{6} \overset{\div 3}{\underset{\div 3}{=}} \dfrac{1}{2}$$

Guided Practice

Solve.

Elena made a spinner with 8 equal parts.
She labeled each part from 1 to 8.

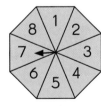

1. How many even numbers are there? Find the probability of landing on an even number when you spin the spinner once.

   There are _____ even numbers.

   The probability of landing on an even number is _____.

2 How many numbers are divisible by 3? Find the probability of landing on a number divisible by 3 when you spin the spinner once.

There are [ ] numbers that are divisible by 3— [ ] and [ ].

The probability of landing on a number divisible by 3 is [ ].

Let's Explore!

The number cards and letter cards shown below are put into a bag.

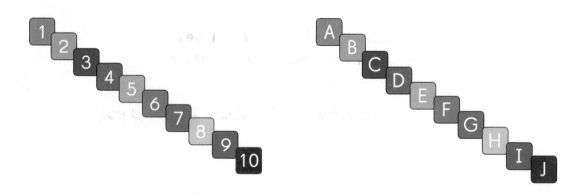

Ask your partner to name 4 different favorable outcomes.
Find the probability of each favorable outcome.
Then switch roles and repeat.

Example

Probability of picking card B = $\dfrac{1}{\text{Number of cards}}$

$= \dfrac{1}{20}$

What do you notice?

Learn **Represent probability on a number line.**

A weather channel forecasted stormy weather on the weekend of an outdoor carnival.

The probability of stormy weather was $\frac{7}{8}$.

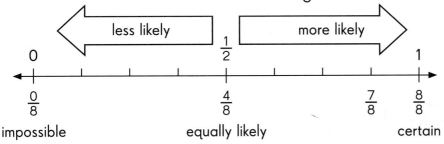

The probability of rain is more likely because $\frac{7}{8}$ is closer to 1 on the number line.

When you write probability as a fraction, the closer the probability of an outcome is to 1, the more likely the outcome is to occur.

Guided Practice

Find each probability as a fraction on the number line. Then describe the likelihood of each outcome as certain, impossible, less likely, more likely, or equally likely.

A bag contains 2 red cubes, 3 yellow cubes, and 3 blue cubes. Find each probability below when you pick one cube from the bag.

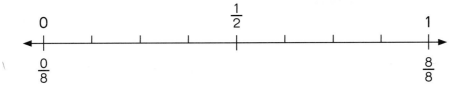

3 Probability of drawing a green cube = ⬚

4 Probability of drawing a yellow cube = ⬚

5 Probability of drawing a red or yellow cube = ⬚

6 Probability of drawing a red, yellow, or blue cube = ⬚

 **Hands-On Activity**

WORK IN PAIRS

Materials:
- Colored markers
- Blank cards
- Blank tally chart

Make 4 red cards, 16 green cards, and 0 yellow cards using the blank cards and colored markers.

STEP 1 Find the probability of drawing each of the three colors.

STEP 2 Label each outcome as *impossible, less likely, equally likely, more likely,* or *certain* based on where the fraction lies on the number line from 0 to 1.

STEP 3 Mix the cards and shuffle them together, face down. Take turns to draw one card from the pack 30 times and record the results in a tally chart. Replace the cards each time. Compare the results with the probabilities you found in **STEP 1**.

Did the less likely outcome happen less often than the more likely outcome? How often did the impossible outcome happen?

Let's Practice

Find each probability as a fraction. Then describe the likelihood of each outcome as certain, impossible, less likely, more likely, or equally likely.

Jake played a dart game at a carnival and won first place. He was asked to pick his prize from a bag that contained the names of these prizes — 4 caps, 3 baseballs, 2 pairs of sneakers, and 1 skateboard.

1 Probability of getting a pair of sneakers =

2 Probability of getting a baseball =

3 Probability of getting a skateboard =

4 Probability of getting a cap or a pair of sneakers =

5 Probability of getting a baseball or a skateboard =

6 Probability of getting a football =

Find each probability as a fraction. Draw a number line and mark a point on the number line for each probability.

Jake's younger sister Shawna came in at third place. She wanted to win a beaded bracelet. Her bag of prizes had the names of these prizes — 4 soft toys, 2 caps, and 1 beaded bracelet.

7 Probability of getting Shawna's favorable outcome =

8 Probability of getting a soft toy =

9 Probability of getting a cap or a beaded bracelet =

10 Probability of getting a beaded bracelet, a cap, or a soft toy =

ON YOUR OWN

**Go to Workbook A:
Practice 5, pages 115–118**

Lesson 5.6 Real-World Problems: Data and Probability

Lesson Objective

- Solve real-world problems involving probability and measures of central tendency.

Learn Solve problems using the mean.

The mean weight of 2 tables is 16 pounds. The weight of one of the tables is 12 pounds. What is the weight of the other table?

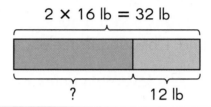

2 × 16 lb = 32 lb

?   12 lb

Total weight of the 2 tables = 16 × 2
                             = 32 lb

Weight of the other table = 32 − 12
                          = 20 lb

The weight of the other table is 20 pounds.

Guided Practice

Solve. Show your work.

1. Mr. Saco bought chicken, fish, and shrimp at a market. The mean weight of the 3 items was 7 pounds. The weight of chicken was 8 pounds and the weight of fish was 4 pounds.
   What was the weight of shrimp that Mr. Saco bought?

   Total weight of chicken, fish, and shrimp Mr. Saco bought = ⬚ × ⬚

   = ⬚ pounds

   Weight of chicken and fish Mr. Saco bought = ⬚ + ⬚

   = ⬚ pounds

Weight of shrimp Mr. Saco bought = [ ] − [ ]

= [ ] pounds

Mr. Saco bought [ ] pounds of shrimp.

2 Kitty bought 20 books at a book fair. The mean cost of 15 of the books was $12. The total cost of the other 5 books was $40.
Find the mean cost of the 20 books.

Total cost of the 15 books = [ ] × [ ]

= [ ]

Total cost of the 20 books = [ ] + [ ]

= [ ]

Mean cost of the 20 books = [ ] ÷ [ ]

= [ ]

The mean cost of the 20 books was [ ].

3 The mean weight of a chicken and a duck is 5 pounds. The duck is 2 pounds heavier than the chicken. Find the weight of the duck.

Total weight of the chicken and duck = [ ] × [ ] = [ ] lb

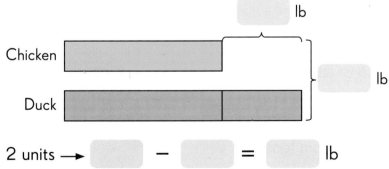

[ ] lb

Chicken

Duck

[ ] lb

2 units → [ ] − [ ] = [ ] lb

1 unit → [ ] ÷ [ ] = [ ] lb

[ ] + [ ] = [ ] lb

The weight of the duck is [ ] pounds.

Jake and five friends went on a trip, and collected 432 rocks altogether. Two of his friends did not count the individual number of rocks they collected. The data that was recorded is shown below.

| 85 | 78 | 93 | 52 | ? | ? |

1 Find the mean number of rocks they collected.

$$\text{Mean} = \frac{432}{6}$$

$$= 72$$

The mean number of rocks they collected is 72.

2 The greatest number of rocks collected is 93, and the range is 47. What is the least number of rocks collected?

Range = Greatest Number − Least Number

$$47 = 93 - ?$$

$$93 - 47 = 46$$

The least number of rocks collected is 46.

3 Find the mode of the set of data.

| 85 | 78 | 93 | 52 | 46 | ? |

To find the mode, first find the unknown item of data.

$$432 - 85 - 78 - 93 - 52 - 46 = 78$$

| 46 | 52 | 78 | 78 | 85 | 93 |

The mode of the set of data is 78.

> Since 46 is not included in the data above, it is one of the missing items of data.

4 Find the median of the set of data.

Arrange the numbers in order, from least to greatest.

| 46 | 52 | 78 | 78 | 85 | 93 |

The median of the set of data is 78.

Guided Practice

Solve. Show your work.

4 A farmer weighed and recorded his crop of pumpkins to the nearest pound as shown in the line plot.

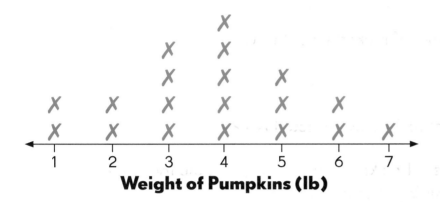 

Weight of Pumpkins (lb)

a What is the mode of the set of data?

b What is the median of the set of data?

c The farmer sold the 4-lb pumpkins at $6 each, the 5-lb pumpkins at $8 each, and the 6-lb pumpkins at $10 each. He kept the rest of the pumpkins. How much money did he earn from the sale?

5 In a mini-bowling competition of four frames per player, Sean scored the following in the first three frames.

Sean's Bowling Score

Frame 1	Frame 2	Frame 3	Frame 4
17	28	25	?

a How many points must he score in the next frame so that he can achieve a mean score of 25?

b How many points must he score in the next frame so that the range of the set of data is 12? Find both possible answers.

Solve problems using a stem-and-leaf plot.

A kindergarten class counted the number of carrots each of its 9 rabbits ate over six months. The stem-and-leaf plot shows the data.

Number of Carrots	
Stem	**Leaves**
5	7 ?
6	3 5 8
7	0 4 4
9	1

$5 \mid 7 = 57$

1 If the mean number of carrots each rabbit ate was 69, find the total number of carrots the rabbits ate over 6 months.

Total number of carrots the rabbits ate over 6 months = 69 × 9
$$= 621$$

The rabbits ate 621 carrots over 6 months.

2 Complete the stem-and-leaf plot by filling in the missing item of data.
621 − 57 − 63 − 65 − 68 − 70 − 74 − 74 − 91 = 59
The missing item of data is 59.

3 Find the mode of the set of data.
The mode of the set of data is 74.

4 Find the median of the set of data.
The median of the set of data is 68.

5 Find the range of the set of data.
The range of the set of data is 91 − 57 = 34.

6 What is the outlier?
The number farthest from the others is 91. The outlier is 91.

Guided Practice

Solve. Show your work.

6 The stem-and-leaf plot shows the lengths of 8 ribbons in inches.

Length of Ribbons (in.)	
Stem	**Leaves**
2	6 8
3	5 6 6 9
4	3
5	3

$2 \mid 6 = 26$

a Which length is the outlier?

b Find the stem which has only even numbers in its leaves column.

c Change some data to make the mode 26 without changing the sum of the lengths.

Solve problems by predicting the likelihood of an outcome.

Jayne has a spinner divided into 12 equal parts. There are 5 yellow parts, 3 green parts, and the remaining 4 parts are blue and red.

1 Jayne spins the spinner once. What color is she most likely to spin?
The color with the greatest number of parts is yellow.
She is most likely to spin yellow.

2 The spinner is equally likely to spin green and one other color. The most unlikely outcome is blue. Draw the spinner with the correct colored parts.

3 Jayne colored one of the yellow parts green. What is the likelihood she will spin red now? Does this change the color she is least likely to spin?
There are now 4 yellow parts, 4 green parts, 3 red parts, and 1 blue part. She is unlikely to spin red. The color she is least likely to spin is still blue.

Guided Practice

Solve. Show your work.

7 A bag contains 15 marbles, of which 6 are red, 5 are blue, and 4 are green. Charlene draws two marbles from the bag.

a If the first marble she draws is red, what is the likelihood that the second marble is blue or red?

b Charlene returns the first two marbles to the bag, and adds two more marbles. She then draws another marble from the bag. What color are the new marbles if each of the following is true?

i The marble she draws is equally likely to be green or red.

ii The marble she draws is most likely to be red.

iii The marble she draws is equally likely to be green or blue.

Solve problems by finding probability as a fraction.

A choir of 32 singers performs at a concert. There are 11 sopranos, 9 tenors, 6 bass, and 6 altos.

After the performance, a singer is randomly chosen to perform a solo.

1 What is the probability that the singer chosen is an alto?

The probability that the singer chosen is an alto is $\frac{6}{32} = \frac{3}{16}$.

2 What is the probability that the singer chosen is a soprano or a tenor?

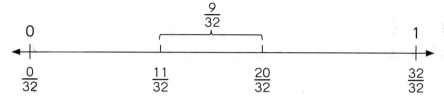

$11 + 9 = 20$

The probability that the singer chosen is a soprano or a tenor is $\frac{20}{32} = \frac{5}{8}$.

Guided Practice
Solve. Show your work.

8 Eighteen students go into a classroom. Eleven of them are girls.
Find each probability as a fraction when the recess bell is rung.

a The first student to come out is a girl.

b The first student to come out is a boy.

c If the first student to come out is a girl, find the probability that the next
student to come out is a boy.

d The probability of the second student to come out being a girl is $\frac{11}{17}$.
Was the first student a boy or a girl?

9 A bag has 6 green marbles and 4 orange marbles. Find the least number
of marbles of either color you would add to make the probability of picking
an orange marble

a $\frac{1}{2}$

b $\frac{1}{3}$

Let's Practice

Solve. Show your work.

1 Mandy bought a turkey burger and a chicken burger. The mean cost of the 2 burgers was $6. The turkey burger cost $5.

a What was the total cost of the 2 burgers?

b How much did the chicken burger cost?

2 The weights of 5 students are shown in the table. However, the total weight of the girls was left out.

Weights of 5 Students

	Students	Total Weight
Girls	Linda, Elsie	?
Boys	Alvin, Chris, George	105 kg

The mean weight of the 5 students is 31 kilograms.

a Find the total weight of the girls.

b Find the mean weight of the girls.

3 Ace Transport has a fleet of 10 trucks. The 7 small trucks use a mean amount of 28 gallons of gas each day. The 3 large trucks use a total amount of 114 gallons each day. What is the mean amount of gas used each day by all 10 trucks?

4 Mr. and Mrs. Soong's mean salary is $2,730. Mrs. Soong earns $230 less than Mr. Soong. How much does each of them earn?

5 Hisham bought 2 action figures with a mean weight of 1,240 grams. The first action figure weighed 80 grams more than the second action figure. What was the weight of the lighter action figure?

6 Katrina sold 4 times as many apples as Bess at a school fair. The two of them sold an average of 285 apples. How many apples did Katrina sell?

7 Matt and his 4 friends collect baseball cards. They have 325 cards altogether. These are the number of baseball cards that 3 of the boys have.

53   73   50   ?   ?

a Find the mean number of cards they have.

b Matt has the largest collection. He has 100 cards. The range of the set of data is 51. What is the smallest collection?

c Jose adds his cards to their collection. There are now 6 friends with 360 cards altogether.
What is the range of this new set of data?

8 A teacher counted the number of peanut butter and jelly sandwiches each of his students had for lunch over a school term. One item of data is missing.

Number of Sandwiches	
Stem	**Leaves**
1	? 6
2	2 2 4 5
3	2 3
4	0 1

1 | 6 = 16

a The mean number of sandwiches each student had was 27. Find the total number of sandwiches.

b What is the missing number in the stem-and-leaf plot?

c Find the mode of the set of data.

d Find the range of the set of data.

e If one of the students was randomly selected, what is the probability that the student had 22 sandwiches?

9 A box has 10 number cards. The cards are numbered 1 to 10. Ann draws a card from the box.

a What is the probability that she draws an even number?

b What is the probability that she draws an odd number that is divisible by 3?

10 A bag contains 1 red cube and 8 blue cubes. Nick picks a cube from the bag.

  a What is the probability that he picks a red cube?

  b If Nick puts the cube back into the bag and picks a cube from the bag again, what is the probability that the second cube is red?

  c If Nick does not put the first cube back and picks a cube from the bag again, what is the probability that the second cube is red?

11 A group of 12 boys, 18 girls, and some adults went to the circus. At a show, 1 of the spectators was randomly selected to perform with the clown. The probability that an adult was selected was $\frac{1}{4}$.

  a How many adults were there?

  b What is the probability that a girl was selected?

12 A group of students count the number of times the letter A appears in their names. The data is shown in the line plot. Each ✗ represents one student.

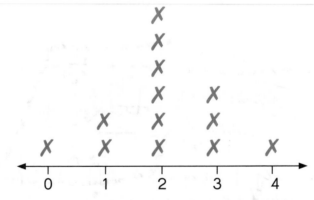

Number of Times Letter A Appears

  a What is the total number of students in the group?

  b What is the mode of this set of data? Is the mode typical of this set of data?

ON YOUR OWN

Go to Workbook A:
Practice 6, pages 119–132

PROBLEM SOLVING

In a Math Olympiad, Team A and Team B each have an equal number of students. The total number of students on each team is less than 10.

The mean score of the students on Team A is 48 points. The mean score of the students on Team B is 62 points. The total score of Team B is 42 points more than that of Team A.

Find the number of students in each team.

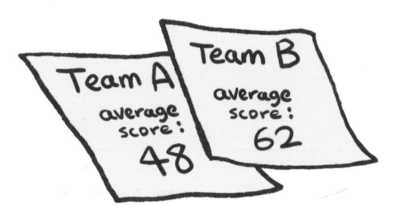

ON YOUR OWN

Go to Workbook A:
Put on Your Thinking Cap!
pages 133–136

Chapter Wrap Up

Study Guide

You have learned...

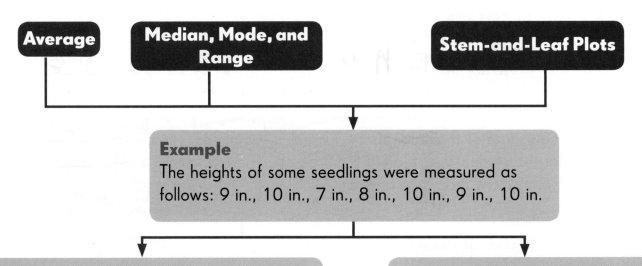

Average **Median, Mode, and Range** **Stem-and-Leaf Plots**

Example

The heights of some seedlings were measured as follows: 9 in., 10 in., 7 in., 8 in., 10 in., 9 in., 10 in.

Find the Mean, Median, Mode, and Range

$$\text{Mean} = \frac{\text{Total number or amount}}{\text{Number of items}}$$

$$= \frac{9 + 10 + 7 + 8 + 10 + 9 + 10}{7}$$

$$= \frac{63}{7} = 9 \text{ in.}$$

When a set of numbers is arranged from least to greatest, the middle number or the mean of the middle numbers is called the median.

7 8 9 ⑨ 10 10 10

Median = 9 in.

The number that appears the greatest number of times is the mode.

7 8 9 9 10 10 10

Mode = 10 in.

The difference between the least and the greatest number in a set of data is the range.

Range = 10 − 7 = 3 in.

Make a Line Plot

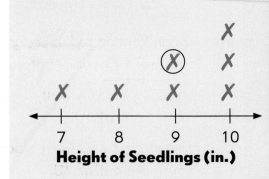

Height of Seedlings (in.)

Make a Stem-and-Leaf Plot

Height of Seedlings	
Stem	**Leaves**
0	7 8 9 9
1	0 0 0

Solve Real-World Problems

BIG IDEAS

▶ Information can be analyzed to find a typical value for a data set.

▶ Data can be analyzed to predict the likelihood of an event happening.

Outcomes

Probability as a Fraction

Example

The spinner is spun once.

Identify the Outcomes of an Experiment

The spinner can land on red, blue, green, or yellow. There are 4 possible outcomes.

Landing on red is equally likely since there are 5 red parts out of 10.

Landing on yellow is less likely since there is only 1 yellow part out of 10.

Landing on blue and landing on green are less likely since there are only 2 parts out of 10 for each.

Landing on black is impossible since there are no black parts.

Landing on blue, green, yellow, or red is certain.

Find the Probability of an Outcome

What is the probability of the spinner landing on each color?

There are 5 red parts.

Probability of landing on red $= \frac{5}{10} = \frac{1}{2}$

There are 2 blue parts.

Probability of landing on blue $= \frac{2}{10} = \frac{1}{5}$

There are no black parts.

Probability of landing on black $= 0$

There is 1 yellow part, 2 green parts, 2 blue parts and 5 red parts.

Probability of landing on blue, green, yellow, or red $= \frac{10}{10} = 1$

Solve Real-World Problems

Chapter Review/Test

Vocabulary

Choose the correct word.

average
mean
median
mode
range
line plot
stem-and-leaf plot
outcome
favorable outcome
probability

1 In a set of data, the number that appears most often is the _____.

2 When a set of data is arranged in order, the middle number or the mean of the two middle numbers is the _____.

3 When a coin is tossed, the _____ of getting tails is $\frac{1}{2}$.

4 The average of a set of data is also called the _____.

5 In a set of data, the difference between the least and the greatest number is the _____.

6 When a coin is tossed, a possible _____ is that the coin lands on heads.

Concepts and Skills
Solve.

Eight students got the following scores on a science quiz.

70	77	85	85	77	95	77	90

7 Find the mean of the set of scores.

8 Draw a stem-and-leaf plot for the scores.

9 Find the median, mode, and range of the scores.

Ten cards numbered 1 to 10 are shuffled.

10 A card with an odd number is drawn. What are the possible outcomes?

11 A card with a number greater than 7 is drawn. What are the possible outcomes?

Find each probability as a fraction.

An eight-sided number cube has the numbers 1, 2, 3, 4, 5, 6, 7, and 8 on it. The number cube is thrown once.
What is the probability of getting

12 a 2?

13 a 2 or a 5?

14 a number less than 4?

15 an even number?

Problem Solving

Solve. Show your work.

16 During one term, Rachel took 2 mathematics tests. Her mean score was 75. She scored 12 points more on the first test than on the second test. How many points did she score on the second test?

17 In a parking lot, there are 16 silver cars, 8 blue cars, and 10 red cars. A car leaves the parking lot. What is the probability that it is

a a silver car?

b a blue car?

c a red car?

d Suppose that the first car that leaves is a silver car. What is the probability that the second car that leaves is not a silver car?

Chapter 6

Fractions and Mixed Numbers

Lessons

BIG IDEAS

▶ Fractions and mixed numbers are used to name wholes and parts of a whole.

▶ Fractions and mixed numbers can be added and subtracted.

220

Recall Prior Knowledge

Representing fractions on a number line

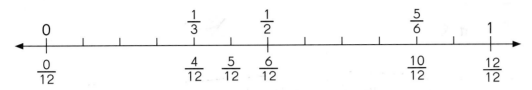

Expressing fractions in simplest form

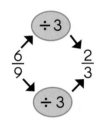

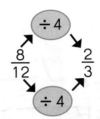

Adding like fractions

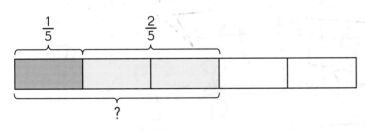

$$\frac{1}{5} + \frac{2}{5} = \frac{3}{5}$$

Subtracting like fractions

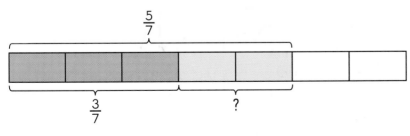

$$\frac{5}{7} - \frac{3}{7} = \frac{2}{7}$$

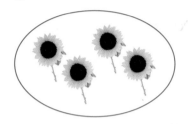 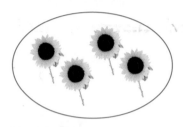 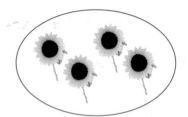
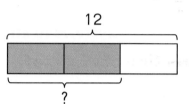
✔ **Quick Check**

Which equivalent fractions are missing on the number lines?
Give your answers in simplest form.

1

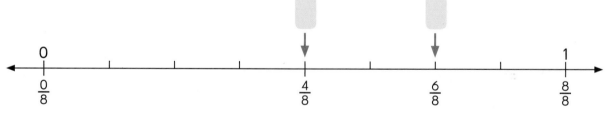

2

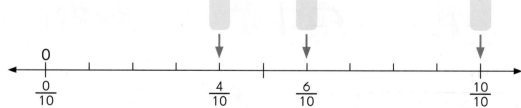

Express each fraction in simplest form.

3 $\frac{9}{12}$ =

4 $\frac{2}{14}$ =

Add or subtract. Express each answer in simplest form.

5 $\frac{3}{7} + \frac{1}{7}$ =

6 $\frac{4}{9} + \frac{2}{9}$ =

7 $\frac{3}{4} - \frac{1}{4}$ =

8 $\frac{5}{8} - \frac{3}{8}$ =

Find the fraction of each set.

9 $\frac{1}{4}$ of 12 =

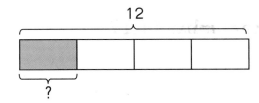

10 $\frac{2}{3}$ of 21 =

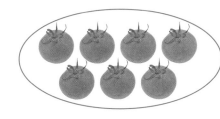

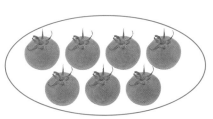

Lesson 6.1 Adding Fractions

Lesson Objectives

- Find equivalent fractions.
- Add unlike fractions.

Vocabulary

numerator	equivalent fraction
denominator	unlike fraction

Learn Add using equivalent fractions.

Lisa ate $\frac{1}{3}$ of a pizza. Katie ate $\frac{1}{6}$ of the same pizza.

What fraction of the pizza did they eat altogether?

First, find an **equivalent fraction** to $\frac{1}{3}$ that has the same **denominator** as $\frac{1}{6}$. Multiply the **numerator** and the denominator by the same number.

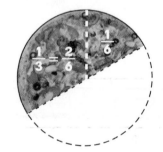

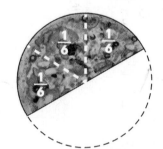

Then add.

$$\frac{1}{3} + \frac{1}{6} = \frac{2}{6} + \frac{1}{6}$$

$$= \frac{3}{6}$$

$$= \frac{1}{2}$$

They ate $\frac{1}{2}$ of the pizza altogether.

Remember to write your answer in simplest form.

To add **unlike fractions**, first change them to fractions with the same denominator. Then add.

Guided Practice

Find the equivalent fraction. Then add.

What fraction is equivalent to $\frac{1}{4}$ and has the same denominator as $\frac{3}{8}$?

1 Add $\frac{1}{4}$ and $\frac{3}{8}$.

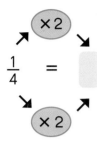

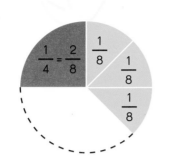 

$$\frac{1}{4} + \frac{3}{8} = \boxed{} + \frac{3}{8}$$

$$= \boxed{}$$

2 Add $\frac{1}{3}$ and $\frac{2}{9}$.

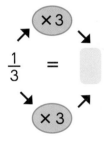

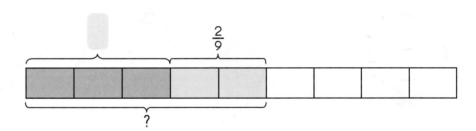

$\frac{2}{9}$

?

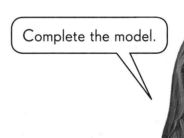

Complete the model.

$$\frac{1}{3} + \frac{2}{9} = \boxed{} + \boxed{}$$

$$= \boxed{}$$

Find each sum.

3  $\frac{1}{2} + \frac{1}{4} = \boxed{} + \frac{1}{4}$

$$= \boxed{}$$

4 $\frac{2}{5} + \frac{3}{10} = \boxed{} + \boxed{}$

$$= \boxed{}$$

Guided Practice

Add. Use models to help you.

5 $\dfrac{5}{12} + \dfrac{1}{3} + \dfrac{1}{12}$

= ▢ + ▢ + ▢

= ▢ = ▢

6 $\dfrac{2}{10} + \dfrac{3}{10} + \dfrac{1}{2}$

= ▢ + ▢ + ▢

= ▢ = ▢

Let's Practice

Find the equivalent fraction. Complete the model. Then add.

1 Add $\dfrac{3}{4}$ and $\dfrac{1}{8}$.

(× 2)

$\dfrac{3}{4} = $ ▢

(× 2)

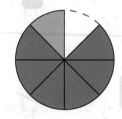

$\dfrac{3}{4} + \dfrac{1}{8} = $ ▢ + ▢

= ▢

Find each sum.

2 $\dfrac{1}{3} + \dfrac{5}{12} = $ ▢ $+ \dfrac{5}{12}$

= ▢

= ▢

(× 4)

$\dfrac{1}{3} = $ ▢

(× 4)

3 $\dfrac{3}{7} + \dfrac{4}{7} = $ ▢

4 $\dfrac{5}{12} + \dfrac{1}{3} = $ ▢

5 $\dfrac{1}{9} + \dfrac{4}{9} + \dfrac{1}{3} = $ ▢

6 $\dfrac{3}{8} + \dfrac{2}{8} + \dfrac{1}{4} = $ ▢

ON YOUR OWN

Go to Workbook A:
Practice 1, pages 137–138

6.2 Subtracting Fractions

Lesson Objectives
- Find equivalent fractions.
- Subtract unlike fractions.

Learn **Subtract using equivalent fractions.**

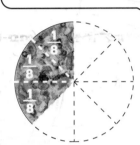

Leo: I ate $\frac{1}{2}$ of a pizza.

Miranda: I ate $\frac{3}{8}$ of the same pizza.

Leo

Miranda

Who ate more? How much more?

First, find an equivalent fraction to $\frac{1}{2}$ that has the same denominator as $\frac{3}{8}$.

Multiply the numerator and denominator by the same number.

$$\frac{1}{2} = \frac{4}{8}$$

$\times 4$ / $\times 4$

Then subtract.

$$\frac{1}{2} - \frac{3}{8} = \frac{4}{8} - \frac{3}{8}$$
$$= \frac{1}{8}$$

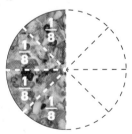

Leo ate $\frac{4}{8}$ of the pizza.

Miranda ate $\frac{3}{8}$ of the pizza.

Leo ate $\frac{1}{8}$ more of the pizza than Miranda.

To subtract unlike fractions, first change them to fractions with the same denominator. Then subtract.

Guided Practice

Find the equivalent fraction. Then subtract.

1 Subtract $\frac{2}{5}$ from $\frac{7}{10}$.

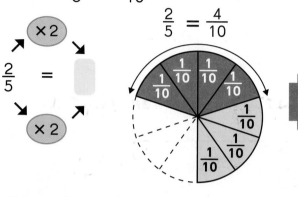

$$\frac{2}{5} = \frac{4}{10}$$

What fraction is equivalent to $\frac{2}{5}$ and has the same denominator as $\frac{7}{10}$?

$$\frac{7}{10} - \frac{2}{5} = \boxed{} - \boxed{}$$

$$= \boxed{}$$

2 Subtract $\frac{7}{12}$ from $\frac{5}{6}$.

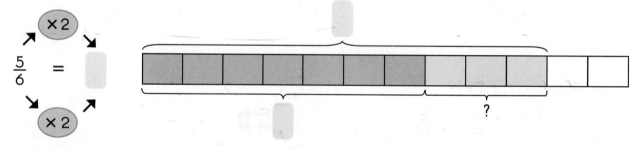

$$\frac{5}{6} - \frac{7}{12} = \boxed{} - \boxed{}$$

$$= \boxed{}$$

$$= \boxed{}$$

Find each difference.

3 $\frac{3}{4} - \frac{1}{2} = \boxed{} - \boxed{} = \boxed{}$

4 $\frac{2}{3} - \frac{5}{9} = \boxed{} - \boxed{} = \boxed{}$

Subtract. Use models to help you.

5 $\dfrac{13}{14} - \dfrac{2}{7} - \dfrac{3}{7} = $ ☐

6 $\dfrac{11}{12} - \dfrac{3}{4} - \dfrac{1}{12} = $ ☐

Let's Practice

Find the equivalent fraction. Complete the model. Then subtract.

1 Subtract $\dfrac{1}{3}$ from $\dfrac{5}{9}$.

$\dfrac{1}{3} = $ ☐

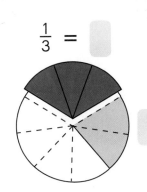

$\dfrac{1}{3}$ ⤢ ×3 ⤥ = ☐

$\dfrac{1}{3} = $ ☐

$\dfrac{5}{9} - \dfrac{1}{3} = $ ☐ $-$ ☐

$= $ ☐

Find each difference.

2 $\dfrac{1}{2} - \dfrac{3}{10} = $ ☐ $- \dfrac{3}{10}$

$= $ ☐

$= $ ☐

$\dfrac{1}{2}$ ⤢ ×5 ⤥ = ☐ ⤡ ×5 ⤤

3 $\dfrac{1}{2} - \dfrac{1}{4} = $ ☐

4 $\dfrac{5}{8} - \dfrac{1}{3} = $ ☐

5 $\dfrac{7}{9} - \dfrac{4}{9} - \dfrac{3}{18} = $ ☐

6 $\dfrac{12}{12} - \dfrac{5}{12} - \dfrac{1}{3} = $ ☐

ON YOUR OWN

**Go to Workbook A:
Practice 2, pages 139–140**

6.3 Mixed Numbers

Lesson Objectives

- Write a mixed number for a model.
- Draw models to represent mixed numbers.

Vocabulary
mixed number

simplest form

Learn **Some situations can be described using a whole number and a fraction.**

1 whole

1 whole

1 half

$$2 + \frac{1}{2} = 2\frac{1}{2}$$

There are $2\frac{1}{2}$ watermelons.

$2\frac{1}{2}$ is a mixed number.

> There are 2 whole watermelons and 1 half watermelon.

When you add a whole number and a fraction, you get a **mixed number**.

Guided Practice

Find the mixed number.

1 Hugo drank 2 bottles of apple juice. Gary drank $\frac{1}{4}$ bottle of apple juice. How many bottles of apple juice did they drink altogether?

$$2 + \frac{1}{4} = \boxed{}$$

They drank $\boxed{}$ bottles of apple juice altogether.

Hands-On Activity

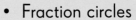
Materials:
- Fraction circles

WORK IN PAIRS

1 Take turns showing the mixed numbers using the fraction circles.

$1\frac{1}{2}$	$2\frac{3}{4}$	$3\frac{3}{4}$	$4\frac{1}{2}$

$5\frac{1}{4}$	$2\frac{3}{5}$	$3\frac{5}{8}$	$4\frac{5}{6}$

2 Take turns drawing pictures to show the mixed numbers.
Your partner will check your answer.

$1\frac{1}{4}$	$2\frac{1}{2}$	$3\frac{3}{4}$	$4\frac{1}{2}$

$3\frac{1}{2}$	$5\frac{1}{4}$	$4\frac{1}{4}$

$2\frac{3}{4}$	$5\frac{1}{2}$

Guided Practice

Find the mixed number that describes each model.

2

1 whole   3 quarters

$1 + \dfrac{3}{4} = $

3

1 whole   1 whole   3 eighths

$2 + \dfrac{3}{8} = $

4

1 whole   1 whole   5 sixths

$2 + \dfrac{5}{6} = $

5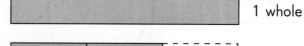

1 whole

2 thirds

$1 + \dfrac{2}{3} = $

6

1 whole

1 whole

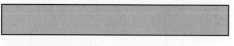 3 quarters

$2 + \dfrac{3}{4} = $

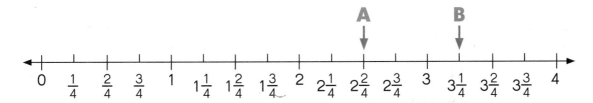

Mixed numbers can be represented on the number line.

What number does each letter represent?

A represents $2\frac{2}{4}$ on the number line.

B represents $3\frac{1}{4}$ on the number line.

You can show mixed numbers on a number line.

Guided Practice

Show each mixed number on the number line.

7 $1\frac{4}{5}$ **8** $2\frac{1}{5}$

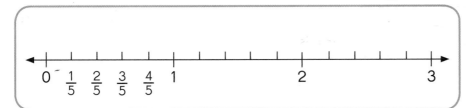

9 $1\frac{1}{2}$ **10** $2\frac{1}{2}$ **11** $3\frac{1}{2}$

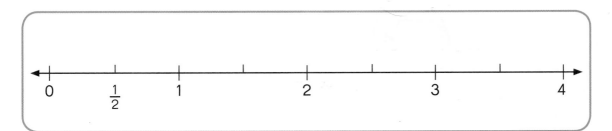

Fractional parts of mixed numbers should be in simplest form.

Simplify the mixed number shown by the shaded parts.

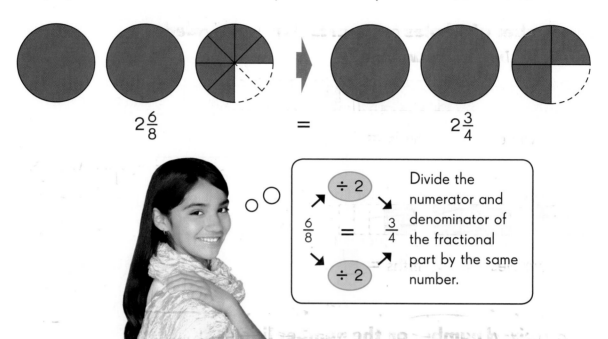

$2\frac{6}{8}$ = $2\frac{3}{4}$

÷ 2

$\frac{6}{8}$ = $\frac{3}{4}$

÷ 2

Divide the numerator and denominator of the fractional part by the same number.

Guided Practice

Express each mixed number in simplest form. Use models to help you.

12 $3\frac{8}{10} = 3\,\rule{1.5em}{1em}$

13 $1\frac{9}{12} = 1\,\rule{1.5em}{1em}$

14 $1\frac{4}{6} = 1\,\rule{1.5em}{1em}$

15 $4\frac{6}{9} = 4\,\rule{1.5em}{1em}$

Find the missing numerator and denominator.

16

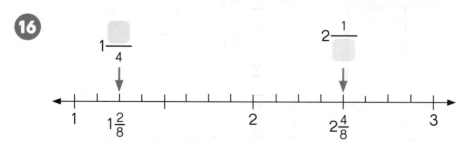

$1\dfrac{\rule{1em}{0.8em}}{4}$ $2\dfrac{1}{\rule{1em}{0.8em}}$

1     $1\frac{2}{8}$ 2 $2\frac{4}{8}$ 3

Let's Practice

**Find the number of wholes and parts that are shaded.
Then write each mixed number.**

1

___ wholes ___ thirds = ___

2

___ wholes ___ fifths = ___

Show each mixed number on the number line.

3 $1\frac{1}{3}$ 　　　　　**4** $2\frac{1}{3}$ 　　　　　**5** $3\frac{2}{3}$

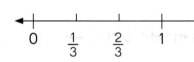

0　　$\frac{1}{3}$　　$\frac{2}{3}$　　1　　　　　2　　　　　3　　　　　4

Write a mixed number to show the amount of milk in each container.

The scales show the amount of milk in each rectangular container.

6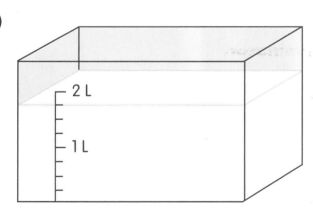

7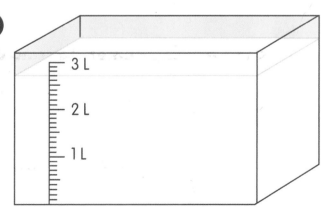

Write two equivalent mixed numbers for the model.

8

Express each mixed number in simplest form.

9 $1\frac{3}{9} = $

$$\boxed{\frac{3}{9} = \frac{1}{3}}$$

10 $5\frac{9}{12} = $

Show each mixed number on the number line.

11 $2\frac{1}{2}$

12 $3\frac{1}{4}$

13 $3\frac{3}{4}$

14 $4\frac{6}{8}$

ON YOUR OWN

Go to Workbook A:
Practice 3, pages 141–146

Lesson 6.4 Improper Fractions

Lesson Objectives

* Write an improper fraction for a model.
* Express mixed numbers as improper fractions.

Vocabulary
improper fraction

Learn Show improper fractions using models.

Mr. Williams has some strips of wire. The wire is measured in $\frac{1}{3}$ meter units.

$\frac{1}{3}$ m

A ▭

$\frac{1}{3}$ = 1 third

$\frac{2}{3}$ m

B ▭

$\frac{2}{3}$ = 2 thirds

$\frac{3}{3}$ m or 1 m

C ▭

$\frac{3}{3}$ = 3 thirds

$$1 = \frac{3}{3}$$
$$= \frac{1}{3} + \frac{1}{3} + \frac{1}{3}$$

$\frac{4}{3}$ m or $1\frac{1}{3}$ m

D ▭

$\frac{4}{3}$ = 4 thirds

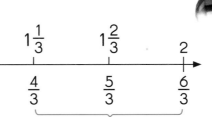

Look at Strip D. It is $1\frac{1}{3}$ meters long.

There are 4 thirds in $1\frac{1}{3}$.

$$1\frac{1}{3} = \frac{1}{3} + \frac{1}{3} + \frac{1}{3} + \frac{1}{3} = \frac{4}{3}$$

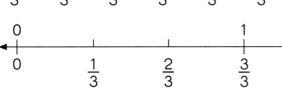

improper fractions

$\frac{4}{3}, \frac{5}{3}$, and $\frac{6}{3}$ are greater than 1.

They are called **improper fractions**.

Continued on next page

Lesson 6.4 Improper Fractions **237**

There are 5 thirds in $1\frac{2}{3}$.

$1\frac{2}{3} = \frac{1}{3} + \frac{1}{3} + \frac{1}{3} + \frac{1}{3} + \frac{1}{3}$

$\qquad = \frac{5}{3}$

There are 5 thirds shaded. One whole circle and $\frac{2}{3}$ of a second circle are shaded.

Guided Practice

Find the missing numbers. Use the models to help you.

1

There are ⬜ fourths in $1\frac{1}{4}$.

$1\frac{1}{4} = $ ⬜ $+$ ⬜ $+$ ⬜ $+$ ⬜ $+$ ⬜

$\qquad = $ ⬜

2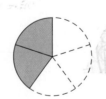

There are ⬜ fifths in $2\frac{2}{5}$.

$2\frac{2}{5} = $

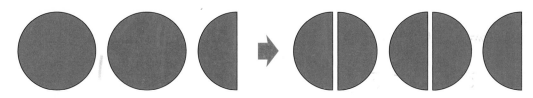

Here is another way to think about improper fractions and mixed numbers.

How many halves are there in $2\frac{1}{2}$?

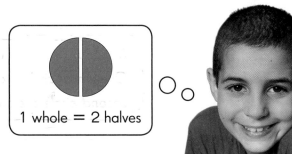

There are 5 halves in $2\frac{1}{2}$.

5 halves $= \frac{5}{2}$

1 whole = 2 halves

Guided Practice

Express each model as an improper fraction.

3

There are fourths in $1\frac{3}{4}$.

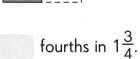 fourths $=$

4 fourths = 1 whole

4

There are 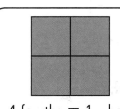 halves in 3.

 halves $=$

5

There are fifths in $1\frac{3}{5}$.

 fifths $=$

Hands-On Activity

Take turns drawing pictures to show the improper fractions.
Your partner will check your answer.

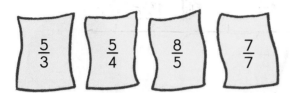

$\frac{5}{3}$ $\frac{5}{4}$ $\frac{8}{5}$ $\frac{7}{7}$

Example

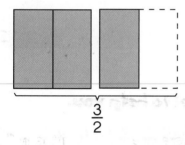

$\frac{3}{2}$

Learn **Express improper fractions in simplest form.**

Simplify the improper fraction shown by the shaded parts.

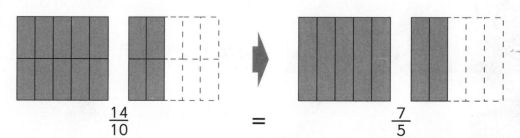

$\frac{14}{10}$ $=$ $\frac{7}{5}$

Guided Practice

Express each improper fraction in simplest form.

6 $\dfrac{15}{6}$ = ☐

7 $\dfrac{26}{12}$ = ☐

8 Find each missing improper fraction.

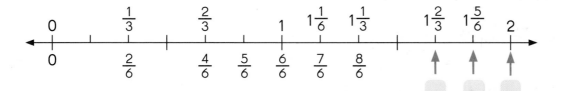

Let's Practice

Find the missing numbers. Use the model to help you.

1

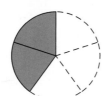

There are ☐ fifths in $1\dfrac{2}{5}$.

$1\dfrac{2}{5}$ = ☐

Trace and shade this shape on a sheet of paper as needed to show the improper fractions.

2 $\dfrac{9}{4}$

3 $\dfrac{11}{8}$

Find the missing improper fraction.

4

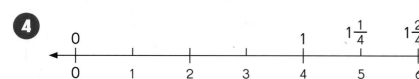

Express each improper fraction in simplest form.

5 $\frac{24}{15}$

6 $\frac{36}{16}$

Show the improper fractions on the number line.

7

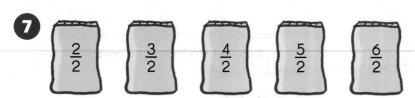

$\frac{2}{2}$ $\frac{3}{2}$ $\frac{4}{2}$ $\frac{5}{2}$ $\frac{6}{2}$

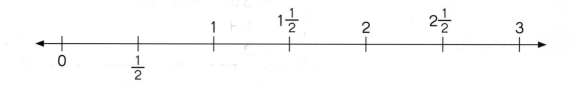

8

1 $\frac{9}{6}$ $\frac{10}{6}$ $\frac{24}{12}$ $\frac{13}{6}$ $\frac{15}{6}$ $\frac{17}{6}$ $\frac{18}{6}$

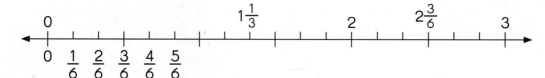

Lesson 6.5 Renaming Improper Fractions and Mixed Numbers

Lesson Objective

- Use multiplication and division to rename improper fractions and mixed numbers.

Vocabulary
fraction bar
division rule
multiplication rule

Learn **Use models to rename improper fractions as mixed numbers or whole numbers.**

Rename $\frac{4}{3}$ as a mixed number.

 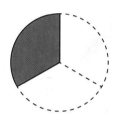

$\frac{4}{3}$ is an improper fraction.

$\frac{4}{3}$ = 4 thirds

= 3 thirds + 1 third

= $\frac{3}{3} + \frac{1}{3}$

= $1 + \frac{1}{3}$

= $1\frac{1}{3}$

Some improper fractions are renamed as whole numbers.

$\frac{6}{3}$ = 6 thirds

= 3 thirds + 3 thirds

= 1 + 1

= 2

Guided Practice

Express the improper fraction as a mixed number or a whole number.

1 $\frac{13}{5}$

$\frac{13}{5}$ = [ ] fifths

= [ ] fifths + [ ] fifths

= [ ] + [ ]

= [ ] + [ ]

= [ ]

Use division to rename improper fractions as mixed numbers or whole numbers.

Rename $\frac{7}{3}$ as a mixed number.

The **fraction bar** means 'divided by'.

$\frac{7}{3}$ means 7 divided by 3.

$$
\begin{array}{r}
\text{number of wholes} \longrightarrow 2 \\
\text{denominator} \longrightarrow 3\overline{)7} \longleftarrow \text{numerator}\\
\underline{6}\\
1
\end{array}
$$

Divide the numerator by the denominator.
$7 \div 3 = 2\,R\,1$
This is the **division rule**.

There are 2 wholes and 1 third in $\frac{7}{3}$.
$\frac{7}{3} = 2\frac{1}{3}$

Some improper fractions are renamed as whole numbers.
$\frac{6}{3}$ is an improper fraction.
$6 \div 3 = 2\,R\,0$
$\frac{6}{3} = 2$

Guided Practice

Express each improper fraction as a mixed number or a whole number. Use the division rule.

2 $\dfrac{15}{4}$ =

3 $\dfrac{13}{6}$ =

4 $\dfrac{25}{5}$ =

Express the improper fraction as a mixed number in simplest form. Then check your answer using the division rule.

5 $\dfrac{15}{9}$

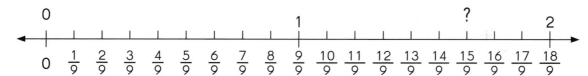

$\dfrac{15}{9}$ = ninths

= ninths + ninths

= +

= +

=

Check

9 ⟌ 15

$15 \div 9 =$ R

$\dfrac{15}{9}$ =

=

Players: **3**
Materials:
- **Number cube**

Roll and Rename!

Work in groups of three.

STEP
1 Player 1 rolls the number cube two times to get two numbers. The player uses the numbers to make an improper fraction.

STEP
2 Player 1 renames the improper fraction as a mixed number.

STEP
3 The other group members check the answer.
Player 1 gets one point if the answer is correct.

STEP
4 Take turns rolling the number cube and writing the numbers.
Play at least 4 rounds.

The player with the highest score wins!

Learn ## Use multiplication to rename a mixed number as an improper fraction.

Rename $3\frac{3}{4}$ as an improper fraction.

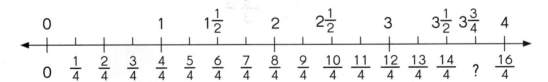

$$3\frac{3}{4} = 3 + \frac{3}{4}$$

$$= \frac{12}{4} + \frac{3}{4}$$

$$= \frac{15}{4}$$

Find how many fourths are in 3.

This is the **multiplication rule**.

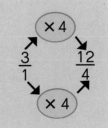

Guided Practice

Express each mixed number as an improper fraction.
Use the multiplication rule.

6 $4\frac{1}{3}$

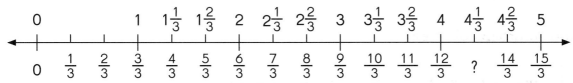

$4\frac{1}{3} = \boxed{} + \frac{1}{3}$

$\phantom{4\frac{1}{3}} = \boxed{} + \frac{1}{3}$

$\phantom{4\frac{1}{3}} = \boxed{}$

$\dfrac{4}{1} \times \boxed{} = \dfrac{\boxed{}}{3}$

$\times \boxed{}$

7 $5\frac{2}{3} = \boxed{} + \frac{2}{3}$

$\phantom{5\frac{2}{3}} = \dfrac{\boxed{}}{3} + \dfrac{2}{3}$

$\phantom{5\frac{2}{3}} = \dfrac{\boxed{}}{3}$

8 $3\frac{1}{5} = \boxed{}$

9 $4\frac{2}{3} = \boxed{}$

Learn **Here is another way to use the multiplication rule.**

Express $3\frac{1}{2}$ as an improper fraction.

First, multiply the whole number by the denominator.

$3 \times 2 = 6$

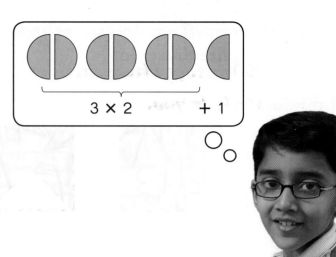

$3 \times 2 \qquad + 1$

Next, add the product to the numerator.

$6 + 1 = 7$

There are 7 halves in $3\frac{1}{2}$.

$3\frac{1}{2} = \frac{7}{2}$

Guided Practice

Express each mixed number as an improper fraction in simplest form.

10 $6\frac{3}{4} = \boxed{} + \frac{3}{4}$

$\phantom{6\frac{3}{4}} = \boxed{} + \frac{3}{4}$

$\phantom{6\frac{3}{4}} = \boxed{}$

Check

$6\frac{3}{4}$

$6 \times \boxed{} = \boxed{}$

$\boxed{} + 3 = \boxed{}$

There are $\boxed{}$ fourths in $6\frac{3}{4}$.

$6\frac{3}{4} = \frac{27}{4}$

11 $1\frac{6}{5} = \boxed{}$

12 $3\frac{2}{5} = \boxed{}$

Let's Practice

Express each improper fraction as a mixed number in simplest form. Use models to help you.

1 $\frac{7}{4}$ =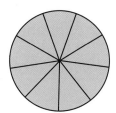

2 $\frac{21}{9}$ =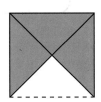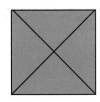

3 $\frac{32}{12}$ =

Express each improper fraction as a mixed number in simplest form. Use the division rule.

4 $\frac{12}{5}$ =

5 $\frac{15}{6}$ =

Express each mixed number as an improper fraction. Use the multiplication rule.

6 $7\frac{2}{5}$ =

7 $3\frac{1}{12}$ =

ON YOUR OWN

Go to Workbook A: Practice 5, pages 151–154

6.6 Renaming Whole Numbers when Adding and Subtracting Fractions

Lesson Objectives

* Add fractions to get mixed-number sums.
* Subtract fractions from whole numbers.

Learn **Add two fractions to get mixed numbers.**

Warren and Drake each had an apple. Warren ate $\frac{7}{8}$ of his apple and Drake ate $\frac{3}{4}$ of his apple. What fraction of the apples did they eat altogether?

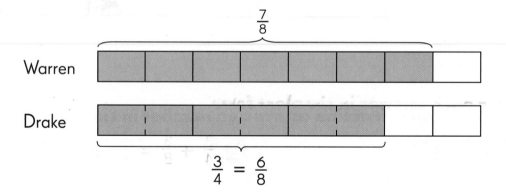

$$\frac{7}{8} \quad \text{(Warren)}$$

$$\frac{3}{4} = \frac{6}{8} \quad \text{(Drake)}$$

$$\frac{7}{8} + \frac{3}{4} = \frac{7}{8} + \frac{6}{8}$$

$$= \frac{13}{8}$$

$$= \frac{8}{8} + \frac{5}{8}$$

$$= 1 + \frac{5}{8}$$

$$= 1\frac{5}{8}$$

$$\boxed{\frac{3}{4} = \frac{6}{8}}$$

They ate $1\frac{5}{8}$ apples altogether.

Learn

Add three fractions to get a mixed number.

Find the sum of $\frac{3}{4}$, $\frac{1}{8}$, and $\frac{5}{8}$.

$$\frac{3}{4} + \frac{1}{8} + \frac{5}{8} = \frac{6}{8} + \frac{1}{8} + \frac{5}{8}$$

$$= \frac{12}{8}$$

$$= \frac{3}{2}$$

$$= 1\frac{1}{2}$$

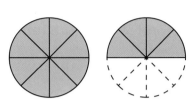

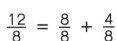

$$\frac{12}{8} = \frac{8}{8} + \frac{4}{8}$$

The sum of $\frac{3}{4}$, $\frac{1}{8}$, and $\frac{5}{8}$ is $1\frac{1}{2}$.

> Always write mixed numbers and fraction answers in simplest form.

Guided Practice

Add. Express each answer in simplest form.

1 $\frac{7}{9} + \frac{2}{3} = \boxed{} + \boxed{}$

$= \boxed{}$

$= \boxed{}$

2 $\frac{3}{4} + \frac{3}{8} = \boxed{} + \boxed{}$

$= \boxed{}$

$= \boxed{}$

3 $\frac{1}{3} + \frac{5}{12} = \boxed{} + \boxed{}$

$= \boxed{}$

$= \boxed{}$

4 $\frac{5}{6} + \frac{1}{12} + \frac{1}{6} = \boxed{} + \boxed{} + \boxed{}$

$= \boxed{}$

$= \boxed{}$

Learn — Subtract fractions from whole numbers.

Rosita had 3 pretzel rods. She ate $\frac{4}{9}$ of one pretzel rod.
What fraction of the pretzel rods are left?

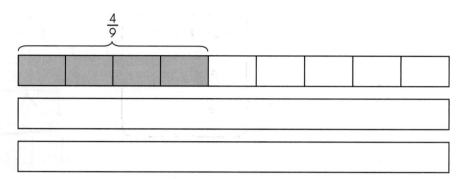

Method 1

$$3 - \frac{4}{9} = 2\frac{9}{9} - \frac{4}{9}$$
$$= 2\frac{5}{9}$$

$$3 = 2 + 1$$
$$= 2 + \frac{9}{9}$$
$$= 2\frac{9}{9}$$

Method 2

$$3 - \frac{4}{9} = \frac{27}{9} - \frac{4}{9}$$
$$= \frac{23}{9}$$
$$= 2\frac{5}{9}$$

$$\begin{array}{r} 2 \\ 9\overline{)2\ 3} \\ 1\ 8 \\ \hline 5 \end{array}$$

There are $2\frac{5}{9}$ pretzel rods left.

$$3 = \frac{9}{9} + \frac{9}{9} + \frac{9}{9}$$
$$= \frac{27}{9}$$

or

$$3 = \frac{3}{1} \overset{\times 9}{=} \frac{27}{9}$$
$$\underset{\times 9}{}$$

Guided Practice

Find the difference.

5 2 and $\frac{3}{8}$.

Method 1

$2 - \frac{3}{8} = \boxed{} - \frac{3}{8}$

$\qquad\ = \boxed{}$

$2 = 1 + 1$

$\ \ = 1 + \boxed{}$

$\ \ = \boxed{}$

Method 2

$2 - \frac{3}{8} = \boxed{} - \frac{3}{8}$

$\qquad\ = \boxed{}$

$\qquad\ = \boxed{}$

$2 = \boxed{} + \boxed{}$

$\ \ = \boxed{}$

or

$2 = \dfrac{2}{\boxed{}} \ \xrightarrow{\times 8} \ \dfrac{\boxed{}}{\boxed{}}$

$\xrightarrow{\times 8}$

6 5 and $\frac{7}{8}$

$\dfrac{5}{1} \ \xrightarrow{\times 8} \ \dfrac{\boxed{}}{8}$

$\xrightarrow{\times 8}$

$\dfrac{\boxed{}}{8} - \dfrac{7}{8} = \dfrac{\boxed{}}{8}$

$\qquad\qquad\ = \boxed{}$

Subtract. Express each answer in simplest form.

7 $4 - \dfrac{5}{7} = \boxed{} - \boxed{} = \boxed{} = \boxed{}$

8 $2 - \dfrac{5}{12} = \boxed{} - \boxed{} = \boxed{} = \boxed{}$

9 $5 - \dfrac{2}{9} = \boxed{} - \boxed{} = \boxed{} = \boxed{}$

10 $3 - \dfrac{8}{9} - \dfrac{1}{3} = \boxed{} - \boxed{} - \boxed{} = \boxed{} = \boxed{}$

Let's Practice

Add. Express each answer in simplest form.

1 $\dfrac{5}{8} + \dfrac{5}{8} = \boxed{}$ **2** $\dfrac{7}{10} + \dfrac{7}{10} = \boxed{}$

3 $\dfrac{4}{9} + \dfrac{2}{3} = \boxed{}$ **4** $\dfrac{5}{12} + \dfrac{3}{4} = \boxed{}$

5 $\dfrac{2}{3} + \dfrac{5}{6} + \dfrac{2}{3} = \boxed{}$ **6** $\dfrac{7}{8} + \dfrac{1}{2} + \dfrac{5}{8} = \boxed{}$

Subtract. Express each answer in simplest form.

7 $2 - \dfrac{3}{7} = \boxed{}$ **8** $5 - \dfrac{2}{3} = \boxed{}$

9 $3 - \dfrac{4}{5} - \dfrac{3}{10} = \boxed{}$ **10** $8 - \dfrac{5}{12} - \dfrac{1}{3} = \boxed{}$

ON YOUR OWN

Go to Workbook A:
Practice 6, pages 155–156

 Lesson 6.7 Fraction of a Set

Lesson Objectives

- Use a bar model to represent a fraction of a set.
- Find a fractional part of a number.

ᴸᵉᵃʳⁿ **Use a model to show a fraction of a set.**

There are 16 cups in the set, and the set of cups is divided

into 4 equal groups. 12 out of the 16 cups in the set are blue.

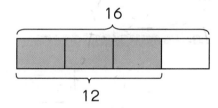

The shaded parts make up $\frac{3}{4}$ of the set.

This means that 3 out of the 4 groups are blue. So, $\frac{3}{4}$ of the cups are blue.

ᴸᵉᵃʳⁿ **Find a fractional part of a number.**

What is $\frac{3}{4}$ of 16?

4 units ⟶ 16

1 unit ⟶ 16 ÷ 4 = 4

3 units ⟶ 3 × 4 = 12

So, $\frac{3}{4}$ of 16 is 12.

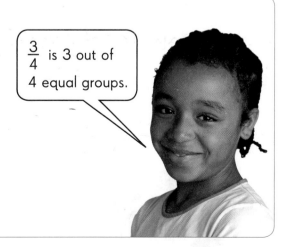

$\frac{3}{4}$ is 3 out of 4 equal groups.

Guided Practice

Find the fraction of the set.

1 Find $\frac{2}{5}$ of 15.

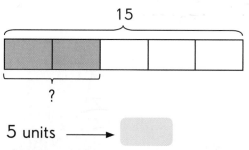

?

Divide 15 into 5 equal parts.
The shaded parts make up $\frac{2}{5}$ of the set.

5 units ⟶ ☐

1 unit ⟶ ☐

2 units ⟶ ☐

So, $\frac{2}{5}$ of 15 is ☐.

2 Find $\frac{2}{3}$ of 6.

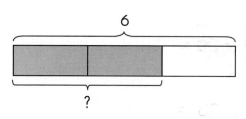

?

The model shows $\frac{2}{3}$ of 6.

3 units ⟶ ☐

1 unit ⟶ ☐

2 units ⟶ ☐

So, $\frac{2}{3}$ of 6 is ☐.

3 $\frac{2}{3}$ of 9 ☐

4 $\frac{3}{5}$ of 30 ☐

Finding a fractional part of a number is the same as multiplying the number by that fraction.

Here is a shorter method to find $\frac{3}{4}$ of 16.

Think of the word "of" as a multiplication symbol.

$$\frac{3}{4} \times 16 = \frac{3 \times 16}{4}$$
$$= \frac{48}{4}$$
$$= 12$$

The product of $\frac{3}{4}$ and 16 can be written as

$\frac{3}{4} \times 16$ or $16 \times \frac{3}{4}$.

Guided Practice

Find the fractional part of each number.

5 $\frac{1}{3}$ of 12 =

6 $\frac{3}{4}$ of 20 =

7 $\frac{4}{5}$ of 25 =

8 $\frac{5}{7}$ of 28 =

Complete.

9 The model shows a set of objects. What fraction of the set does the shaded part show?

21

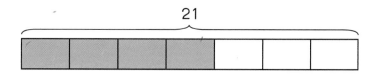

The shaded part shows   of   .

Let's Practice

Solve.

1 Which group shows $\frac{3}{4}$ of the shapes colored? Group [____]

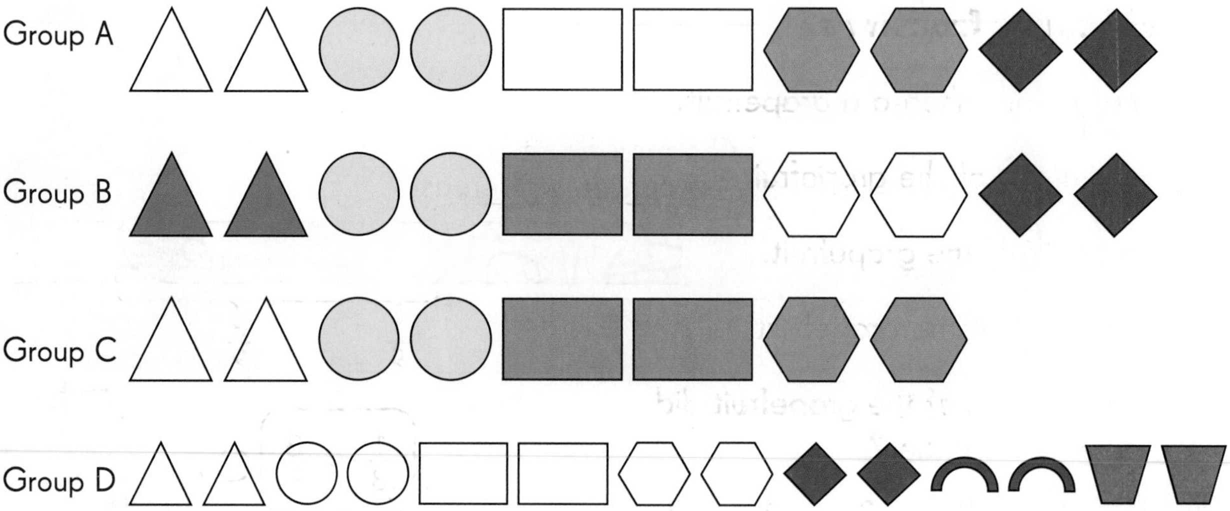

Group A △ △ ● ● ▭ ▭ ⬡ ⬡ ◆ ◆

Group B ▲ ▲ ● ● ▮ ▮ ⬡ ⬡ ◆ ◆

Group C △ △ ● ● ▮ ▮ ⬡ ⬡

Group D △ △ ○ ○ ▭ ▭ ⬡ ⬡ ◆ ◆ ⌒ ⌒ ▽ ▽

Use models to find the fractional part of each number.
Use multiplication to check your answer.

2 $\frac{2}{5}$ of 30 = [____]

3 $\frac{4}{9}$ of 45 = [____]

4 $\frac{3}{8}$ of 64 = [____]

5 $\frac{6}{11}$ of 55 = [____]

ON YOUR OWN

Go to Workbook A:
Practice 7, pages 157–160

Real-World Problems: Fractions

Lesson Objective

• Solve real-world problems involving fractions.

Learn **Add three fractions.**

Three friends shared a grapefruit.

Elena ate $\frac{1}{3}$ of the grapefruit.

Lee ate $\frac{1}{9}$ of the grapefruit.

Sara ate $\frac{3}{9}$ of the grapefruit.

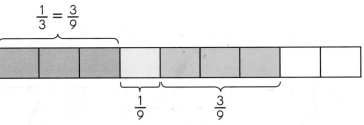

What fraction of the grapefruit did
they eat altogether?

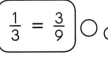

$$\frac{1}{3} + \frac{1}{9} + \frac{3}{9} = \frac{3}{9} + \frac{1}{9} + \frac{3}{9}$$

$$= \frac{7}{9}$$

Elena, Lee, and Sara ate $\frac{7}{9}$ of the grapefruit.

Guided Practice

Solve. Show your work.

1 Mrs. Long needed sugar for a recipe. She had $\frac{1}{4}$ cup of sugar in

an open package. Mrs. Long added another $\frac{7}{8}$ cup of sugar from a

new package. How much sugar did she use in all?

$$\frac{1}{4} + \frac{7}{8} = \boxed{} + \frac{7}{8}$$

$$= \boxed{}$$

$$= \boxed{}$$

She used ☐ cups of sugar in all.

2 Sean, Roger, and Damon each drank different amounts of milk one day.

Sean drank $\frac{5}{6}$ quart of milk. Roger drank $\frac{7}{12}$ quart of milk and

Damon drank $\frac{11}{12}$ quart of milk.

How much milk did they drink altogether?

$$\frac{5}{6} + \frac{7}{12} + \frac{11}{12} = \boxed{} + \frac{7}{12} + \frac{11}{12}$$

$$= \boxed{}$$

$$= \boxed{}$$

$$= \boxed{}$$

They drank $\boxed{}$ quarts of milk altogether.

Learn **Subtract fractions from whole numbers.**

Cheryl and Dennis made a pumpkin pie.

Cheryl ate $\frac{2}{5}$ of the pie.

Dennis ate $\frac{3}{10}$ of the pie.

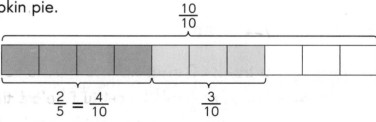

$$\frac{10}{10}$$

$$\frac{2}{5} = \frac{4}{10} \qquad \frac{3}{10}$$

What fraction of the pumpkin pie was left?

$$1 - \frac{2}{5} - \frac{3}{10} = \frac{10}{10} - \frac{4}{10} - \frac{3}{10}$$

$$= \frac{3}{10}$$

$$\boxed{\frac{2}{5} = \frac{4}{10}}$$

$\frac{3}{10}$ of the pumpkin pie was left.

A craft store has a 9-yard spool of ribbon. In the morning, a customer buys $\frac{1}{5}$ yard of ribbon from the spool. In the afternoon, another customer buys $\frac{7}{10}$ yard of ribbon from the spool. How much ribbon is left?

Method 1

$$9 - \frac{1}{5} - \frac{7}{10} = 8\frac{10}{10} - \frac{1}{5} - \frac{7}{10}$$

$$= 8\frac{10}{10} - \frac{2}{10} - \frac{7}{10}$$

$$= 8\frac{1}{10}$$

Method 2

$$\frac{1}{5} + \frac{7}{10} = \frac{2}{10} + \frac{7}{10}$$

$$= \frac{9}{10}$$

$$9 - \frac{9}{10} = 8\frac{10}{10} - \frac{9}{10}$$

$$= 8\frac{1}{10}$$

$8\frac{1}{10}$ yards of ribbon are left.

Guided Practice

Solve. Show your work.

③ Terry had to travel 12 miles from Town A to Town B. He traveled $\frac{5}{8}$ mile by bus. Then he traveled another $\frac{1}{4}$ mile by car just before the car broke down. How far was he from Town B when the car broke down?

Method 1

$$12 - \frac{5}{8} - \frac{1}{4} = 11\boxed{} - \frac{5}{8} - \frac{1}{4}$$

$$= \boxed{} - \frac{5}{8} - \boxed{}$$

$$= \boxed{}$$

Method 2

$$\boxed{} + \boxed{} = \boxed{} + \boxed{}$$

$$= \boxed{}$$

$$\boxed{} - \boxed{} = \boxed{} - \boxed{}$$

$$= \boxed{}$$

He was $\boxed{}$ miles from Town B when the car broke down.

Find the fraction of a set.

Learn **Find the fraction of a set.**

There are 9 roses in a vase. Of the 9 roses, 6 are red and the rest are yellow.

What fraction of the roses are red?

6 out of 9 roses are red.

$\frac{2}{3}$ of the roses are red.

What fraction of the roses are yellow?

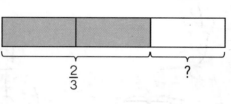

$\frac{2}{3}$?

6 out of 9 in simplest form is $\frac{2}{3}$.

$1 - \frac{2}{3} = \frac{3}{3} - \frac{2}{3}$

$\phantom{1 - \frac{2}{3}} = \frac{1}{3}$

$\frac{1}{3}$ of the roses are yellow.

Guided Practice

Solve. Show your work.

4 Alma had a 1-meter length of string. She cut off an 18-centimeter piece.

a What fraction of the string is cut off?

18 out of 100 is $\frac{18}{100}$.

$\frac{18}{100} = $ ▢

▢ of the string is cut off.

Convert 1 meter to 100 centimeters.

b What fraction of the string is left?

$1 - ▢ = ▢ - ▢ = ▢$

▢ of the string is left.

^{Learn} **Use multiplication and division to find the total.**

Judy bought a few pieces of fruit. $\frac{2}{5}$ of them were pears.

She bought 12 pears.

How many pieces of fruit did Judy buy altogether?

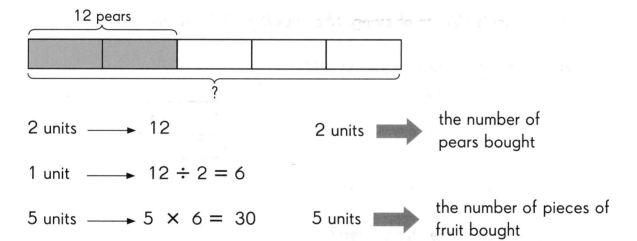

2 units $\longrightarrow$ 12   2 units the number of pears bought

1 unit $\longrightarrow$ 12 ÷ 2 = 6

5 units $\longrightarrow$ 5 × 6 = 30   5 units the number of pieces of fruit bought

Judy bought 30 pieces of fruit altogether.

Guided Practice

Solve. Show your work.

5 Vincent spent $\frac{4}{7}$ of his money on a pair of shoes.
The shoes cost $48. How much money did he have at first?

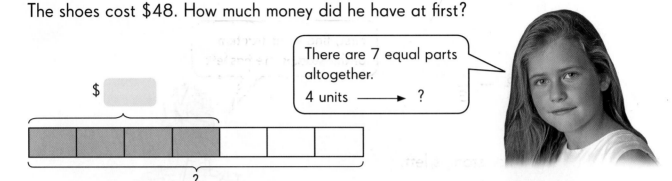

$ [   ]

There are 7 equal parts altogether.

4 units ——→ ?

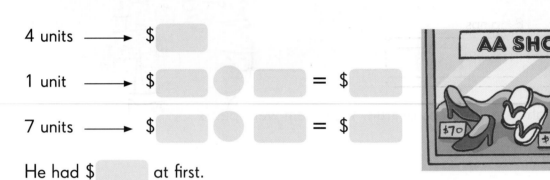

?

4 units ——→ $ [   ]

1 unit ——→ $ [   ] ⚪ [   ] = $ [   ]

7 units ——→ $ [   ] ⚪ [   ] = $ [   ]

He had $ [   ] at first.

AA SHOE SHOP

$48 $70 $20 $80

6 A pitcher contains a liquid mixture of water and lemon juice.
The water makes up $\frac{2}{5}$ of the weight of the liquid mixture. There are 25 ounces of
water in the pitcher. How much lemon juice is in the pitcher?

2 units ——→ [   ]

1 unit ——→ [   ]

3 units ——→ [   ]

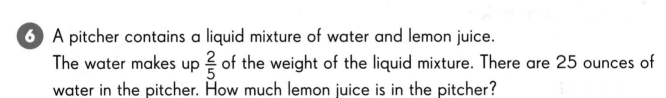

25 ounces

?

= [   ]

= [   ] ounces

The weight of lemon juice in the jug is [   ] ounces.

Use multiplication and division rules to find a fraction of a set.

Sally had 18 stamps. She sold $\frac{1}{3}$ of them.
How many stamps does she have left?

Method 1

$$1 - \frac{1}{3} = \frac{3}{3} - \frac{1}{3}$$
$$= \frac{2}{3}$$

She has $\frac{2}{3}$ of her stamps left.

First, find what fraction of the stamps she has left.

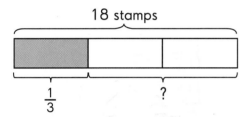

18 stamps

$\frac{1}{3}$?

$$\frac{2}{3} \times 18 = \frac{36}{3}$$
$$= 12$$

She has 12 stamps left.

Method 2

3 units ⟶ 18
1 unit ⟶ 18 ÷ 3 = 6   1 unit the number of stamps
She sold 6 stamps.   Sally sold

2 units ⟶ 2 × 6 = 12   2 units the number of stamps
                                          Sally has left

Sally has 12 stamps left.

Guided Practice

Solve. Show your work.

7 Dante had $50. He used $\frac{3}{5}$ of it to buy a jacket. How much money does he have left?

Method 1

5 units ⟶ [ ]

1 unit ⟶ $ [ ] ◯ [ ] = $ [ ]

2 units ⟶ $ [ ] ◯ [ ] = $ [ ]

He has $ [ ] left.

$ [ ]

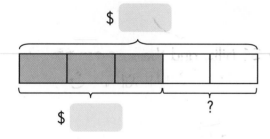

$ [ ]   ?

Method 2

$\frac{3}{5}$ of $50 = [ ] × $ [ ]

$= \$\dfrac{[\ ]}{[\ ]}$

$= \$ [\ ]$

Dante spent $ [ ] on the jacket.

$ [ ] − $ [ ] = $ [ ]

He has $ [ ] left.

Let's Practice

Solve. Show your work.

1. Jane measures the length of three ropes. Rope A is $\frac{1}{2}$ meter long. Rope B is $\frac{5}{8}$ meter long and Rope C is $\frac{3}{8}$ meter long. What is the total length of the three ropes?

2. Mark is making salad dressing. He mixes $\frac{3}{4}$ liter of olive oil with $\frac{11}{12}$ liter of vinegar.

   a. How much dressing does he make?

   b. If he has 8 liters of olive oil to begin with, how much is left after making the dressing?

3. Celine has 10 bills in her wallet. She has four $1 bills, and the rest are $5 bills.

   a. What fraction of the bills are $1 bills?

   b. What fraction of the bills are $5 bills?

4. Mrs. Jackson bought 24 pounds of flour. She used $\frac{3}{8}$ of it to make bread.

   a. How much flour did she use?

   b. How much flour does she have left?

5. Lianne spent a total of $36 on a textbook and a storybook.

   The textbook cost $\frac{4}{9}$ of the total amount spent.

   How much money did Lianne spend on the storybook?

6. Daryl bought some fish for his tank, $\frac{1}{4}$ of which were angelfish.

   The rest were guppies. He bought 32 angelfish.

   How many fish did he buy altogether?

ON YOUR OWN

Go to Workbook A:
Practice 8, pages 161–168

PROBLEM SOLVING

1 The model shows $\frac{3}{4}$ of a fraction strip shaded.
How many of the shaded parts must be erased so that
the remaining shaded parts are $\frac{3}{8}$ of the strip?

Try drawing the model in another way.

Put On Your Thinking Cap!

PROBLEM SOLVING

(2) Jessie had a whole graham cracker.

Minah had only part of another graham cracker.

Jessie gave $\frac{1}{4}$ of her graham cracker to Minah.

In the end, both girls had the same fractional part of

a graham cracker.

What fraction of a graham cracker did Minah have at first?

Jessie

Minah

Here are 2 equal bars to show that both of them had an equal portion of a graham cracker in the end.

Work backward to find the fraction of the graham cracker Minah had at first.

ON YOUR OWN

**Go to Workbook A:
Put on Your Thinking Cap!
pages 169–170**

Chapter Wrap Up

Study Guide
You have learned...

Adding and Subtracting Unlike Fractions

To add and subtract unlike fractions, first change them to fractions with the same denominator. Then, add or subtract.

Adding Fractions	Subtracting Fractions
$\frac{7}{12} + \frac{1}{4}$	$\frac{7}{15} - \frac{2}{5}$

$\frac{1}{4} \overset{\times 3}{\underset{\times 3}{=}} \frac{3}{12}$ $\frac{2}{5} \overset{\times 3}{\underset{\times 3}{=}} \frac{6}{15}$

$\frac{7}{12} + \frac{3}{12} = \frac{10}{12} = \frac{5}{6}$ $\frac{7}{15} - \frac{6}{15} = \frac{1}{15}$

Solve Real-World Problems

Emily drank $\frac{1}{6}$ quart of milk, and Shane drank $\frac{2}{3}$ quart of milk. How much milk did they drink altogether?

$\frac{1}{6} + \frac{2}{3} = \frac{1}{6} + \frac{4}{6}$
$= \frac{5}{6}$

They drank $\frac{5}{6}$ quart of milk altogether.

Mixed Numbers

$2\frac{1}{4}$ is a mixed number. It consists of a whole number, 2, and a fraction, $\frac{1}{4}$.

Improper Fraction

$\frac{5}{5}$, $\frac{6}{5}$, and $\frac{7}{5}$ are improper fractions. They are equal to greater than 1.

Renaming Improper Fractions and Mixed Numbers

$2\frac{1}{4} \longleftrightarrow \frac{9}{4}$

$2\frac{1}{4} = 2 + \frac{1}{4}$
$= \frac{8}{4} + \frac{1}{4}$
$= \frac{9}{4}$

or

First, multiply the whole number by the denominator.
$2 \times 4 = 8$
Next, add the result to the numerator 1.
$8 + 1 = 9$
There are 9 quarters in $2\frac{1}{4}$.

$2\frac{1}{4} = \frac{9}{4}$

$\frac{9}{4} = \frac{8}{4} + \frac{1}{4}$
$= 2 + \frac{1}{4}$
$= 2\frac{1}{4}$

or

$\frac{9}{4} = 9 \div 4 = 2$ R

number of whole

denominator $\longrightarrow 4\overline{)9}^{\,2}$

numerator

$\frac{9}{4} = 2\frac{1}{4}$

BIG IDEAS

▶ Fractions and mixed numbers are used to name wholes and parts of a whole.
▶ Fractions and mixed numbers can be added and subtracted.

Renaming Whole Numbers when Adding and Subtracting Fractions

Add fractions to get a sum greater than 1.

$$\frac{3}{4} + \frac{1}{8} + \frac{3}{8}$$
$$= \frac{6}{8} + \frac{1}{8} + \frac{3}{8}$$
$$= \frac{10}{8}$$
$$= 1\frac{2}{8}$$
$$= 1\frac{1}{4}$$

Subtract fractions from a whole number.

$$2 - \frac{1}{6} - \frac{5}{12}$$
$$= 1\frac{12}{12} - \frac{2}{12} - \frac{5}{12}$$
$$= 1\frac{5}{12}$$
or
$$2 - \frac{1}{6} - \frac{5}{12}$$
$$= \frac{24}{12} - \frac{2}{12} - \frac{5}{12}$$
$$= \frac{17}{12}$$
$$= 1\frac{5}{12}$$

Fraction of a Set

In a group of 12 flowers, 8 are pink. So, $\frac{2}{3}$ of the flowers are pink.

Solve Real-World Problems

Eliza spent $35, which is $\frac{7}{9}$ of the amount that she had. How much money did she have at first?

7 units ⟶ $35

1 unit ⟶ $5

9 units ⟶ $45

She had $45.

Solve Real-World Problems

A baker had 5 pounds of flour. He used $\frac{3}{4}$ pound to make muffins and $\frac{1}{8}$ pound to make bread. How much flour is left?

$$5 - \frac{3}{4} - \frac{1}{8} = 4\frac{8}{8} - \frac{6}{8} - \frac{1}{8}$$
$$= 4\frac{1}{8}$$

$4\frac{1}{8}$ pounds of flour are left.

Chapter Review/Test

Vocabulary

Choose the correct word.

> numerator
> denominator
> unlike fractions
> equivalent fraction
> fraction bar
> mixed number
> improper fraction
> multiplication rule
> division rule

1 The ⬚ appears above the fraction bar, and the ⬚ appears below it.

2 Two fractions that have different denominators are called ⬚ .

3 The multiplication rule is used to rename a ⬚ as an ⬚ .

Concepts and Skills

Find the missing improper fractions and mixed numbers.

4

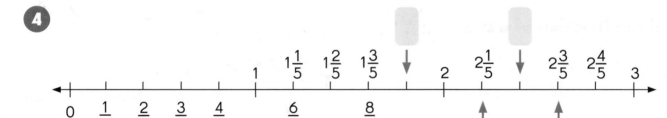

Use a model to represent the mixed number.
Then express the mixed number as an improper fraction.

5 $2\frac{1}{2}$

There are ⬚ halves in $2\frac{1}{2}$.

$2\frac{1}{2}$ = ⬚

Express each mixed number as an improper fraction.

6 $3\frac{1}{4}$ =

7 $2\frac{1}{3}$ =

Express each improper fraction as a mixed number.

8 $\frac{7}{4}$ =

9 $\frac{9}{2}$ =

Add or subtract.

10 $\frac{4}{5} + \frac{3}{10}$ =

11 $\frac{5}{7} - \frac{1}{14}$ =

12 $\frac{1}{3} + \frac{5}{6} + \frac{2}{3}$ =

13 $1 - \frac{2}{5} - \frac{1}{10}$ =

14 $\frac{4}{9} + \frac{2}{3} + \frac{1}{3}$ =

15 $3 - \frac{5}{6} - \frac{1}{12}$ =

Find the fraction of a set.

16 $\frac{5}{6}$ of 48 =

17 $\frac{4}{7}$ of 49 =

Problem Solving

Solve. Show your work.

18 Mary has 18 beads, and 6 of them are red. The rest are blue. What fraction of the beads are blue?

19 Rory spends $\frac{1}{5}$ hour cleaning the table, $\frac{3}{10}$ hour washing dishes, and $\frac{4}{5}$ hour reading a book. How many hours does she spend doing all these activities?

20 John has $24. He uses $\frac{2}{3}$ of his money to buy a pair of shoes. How much money is left?

Glossary

A ————————

- **average**

  $$\text{Average or mean} = \frac{\text{Total number or amount}}{\text{Number of items}}$$

  3 students collect a total of 12 shells. The average number of shells collected by each student is 12 ÷ 3, or 4 shells.

C ————————

- **certain outcome**

  An outcome that will definitely occur is a certain outcome.

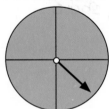

  It is certain that the spinner will land on blue.

- **column**

  Data in a table is organized vertically by columns.

  column ⌐————→ **Popular Types of Food**

Age group	Italian	Mexican	Chinese
Under 12	21	16	9
From 12 to 18	24	29	13
Over 18	35	26	28

- **common factor**

  A factor that is shared by two or more numbers is a common factor.

  Factors of 9: ⓵, ⓷, and 9

  Factors of 12: ⓵, 2, ⓷, 4, 6, and 12

  1 and 3 are common factors of 9 and 12.

- **common multiple**

  A number that is a multiple of two or more numbers is a common multiple.

  Multiples of 4: 4, 8, ⑫, 16, 20, ㉔ ...

  Multiples of 6: 6, ⑫, 18, ㉔ ...

  The common multiples of 4 and 6 are 12, 24 ...

- **composite number**

  A composite number has more than 2 different factors.
  6 is a composite number, because it has 4 factors: 1, 2, 3, and 6.

D

- **data**

  A set of data is a set of information, usually numbers.
  Data can be represented in graphs, tables, tally charts, line plots, and stem-and-leaf plots.

- **denominator**

  The denominator of a fraction shows how many equal parts the whole or the set is divided into.

  $\frac{7}{9}$ ◄——— denominator

   There are 9 equal parts.

- **division rule**

  The division rule can be used to rename an improper fraction as a mixed number. $\frac{9}{4}$ means 9 divided by 4.

  $9 \div 4 = 2 \text{ R } 1$

  There are 2 wholes and 1 fourth in $\frac{9}{4}$.

  $\frac{9}{4} = 2\frac{1}{4}$

 E ————————————

- **equally likely outcomes**

  Outcomes which have the same chance or probability of occuring are described as equally likely outcomes.

  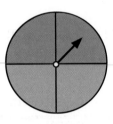

  It is equally likely that the spinner will land on orange or on purple.

  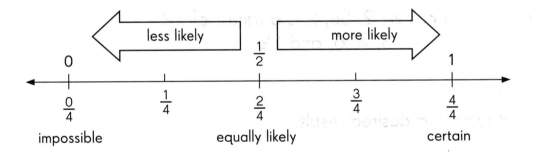

- **equivalent fraction**

  Equivalent fractions have the same value.

  $\frac{6}{18}$ and $\frac{1}{3}$ are equivalent fractions.

  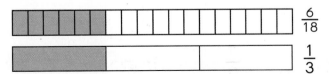

- **estimate**

  An estimate is a number close to the exact number.
  An estimate of the sum of 214 and 545 is 700.

- **expanded form**

  The expanded form of a number shows the number as the sum of
  the values of its digits. For example, 51,678 is the sum of

  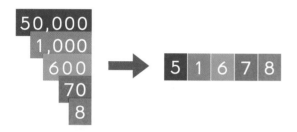

  Expanded form: 50,000 + 1,000 + 600 + 70 + 8

F

- **factor**

  12 can be divided exactly by 2. So, 2 is a factor of 12.
  The factors of 12 are 1, 2, 3, 4, 6, and 12.

- **favorable outcome**

  A favorable outcome is a desired result.

  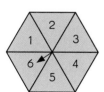

  Jay wants to land on an even number.
  The numbers 2, 4, and 6 are favorable outcomes.

- **fraction bar**

  The fraction bar means 'divided by'. $\frac{7}{9}$ ◄——— fraction bar

- **front-end estimation**

  Front-end estimation uses the leading digits in numbers to make an estimate.

  ⑨,782 − ⑤,411

  9,000 − 5,000 = 4,000

  G ——————————

- **greater than (>)**

  The number that is farther to the right on a number line is greater than the other.

  33,450   **28,539**

  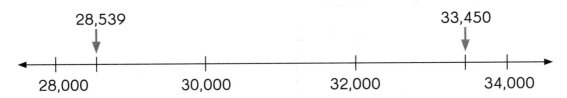

  33,450 is greater than 28,539.
  33,450 > 28,539

- **greatest**

  The number that is farthest to the right on a number line is the greatest of three or more numbers.

  33,450   **28,539**   **31,707**

  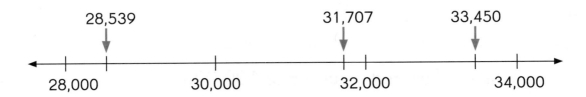

  33,450 is the greatest number.

- **greatest common factor**

  Factors of 12: ①, ②, 3, ④, 6, and 12

  Factors of 16: ①, ②, ④, 8, and 16

  The common factors of 12 and 16 are 1, 2, and 4.
  The greatest common factor of 12 and 16 is 4.

H

- **horizontal axis**

  The horizontal axis on a graph is the line that runs straight across from left to right.

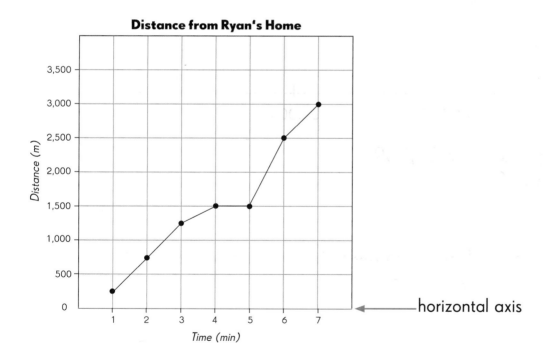

- **hundred thousand**

  10 ten thousands = 1 hundred thousand or 100,000

I

- ## impossible outcome

  An outcome that will definitely not occur is an impossible outcome.

  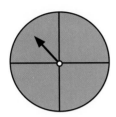

  It is impossible that the spinner will land on red.

- ## improper fraction

  An improper fraction has a numerator that is greater than its denominator. It represents a fraction that is greater than 1.

  $\frac{12}{7}$ and $\frac{4}{3}$ are improper fractions.

- ## intersection

  An intersection is the area of a table where a row and column meet.

column

Popular Types of Food

Age group	Italian	Mexican	Chinese
Under 12	21	16	9
From 12 to 18	24	29	13
Over 18	35	26	28

Row

intersection

L

- ## least

  The number that is farthest to the left on a number line is the least of three or more numbers.

  33,450   **28,539**   **31,707**

  28,539 is the least number.

- ## least common multiple

  Multiples of 3: 3, 6, 9, (12), 15, 18, 21, (24) ...
  Multiples of 4: 4, 8, (12), 16, 20, (24) ...
  The common multiples of 3 and 4 are 12, 24 ...
  The least common multiple of 3 and 4 is 12.

- ## less likely outcome

  If the probability of an outcome is between 0 and $\frac{1}{2}$, it is less likely to occur.

  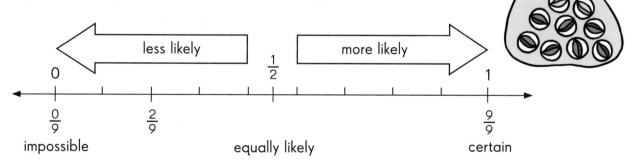

  It is less likely that a yellow marble will be drawn from the bag.

- ## less than (<)

  The number that is farther to the left on a number line is less than the other.

  56,498   **52,731**

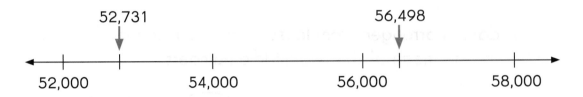

  52,731 is less than 56,498. 52,731 < 56,498

- ## line graph

  A line graph shows how data changes over time.

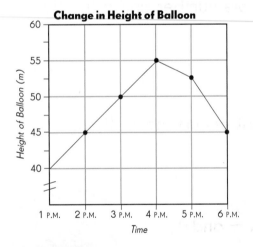

- ## line plot

  A line plot shows the frequency of data on a number line.
  Each X represents one occurrence.

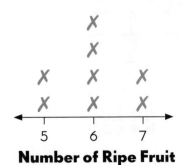

Frequency is the number of times an item of data occurs.

M

- **mean**

  See **average**.

- **median**

  When a set of data is arranged from least to greatest, the median is the middle number, or the mean of the two middle numbers.

  4   7   7   (8)   9   9   9

  Median = 8

  2   2   4   (6   8)   8   9   10

  $$\text{Median} = \frac{6 + 8}{2} = 7$$

- **mixed number**

  A mixed number represents the sum of a whole number and a fraction. $2\frac{3}{4}$ is a mixed number.

- **mode**

  The mode of a set of data is the number that occurs most often.

  4   7   7   8   (9)   (9)   (9)   Mode = 9

- **more likely outcome**

  If the probability of an outcome is between $\frac{1}{2}$ and 1, it is more likely to occur.

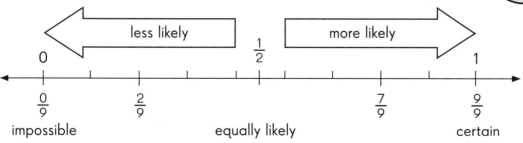

It is more likely that a blue marble will be drawn from the bag.

- **more than**

  17,890 people is more than 17,000 people.
  890 more than 17,000 is 17,890.

- **multiple**

  A multiple of a number is the product of the number and any other whole number except zero.
  The multiples of 7 are 7, 14, 21, 28, 35...

- **multiplication rule**

  The multiplication rule can be used to rename a mixed number as an improper fraction.

  $$3\frac{3}{4} = 3 + \frac{3}{4}$$
  $$= \frac{12}{4} + \frac{3}{4}$$
  $$= \frac{15}{4}$$

N

- **numerator**

  The numerator of a fraction shows the number of equal parts of the whole or set that you are counting.

  $\frac{7}{9}$ ⟵——— numerator

  7 of the 9 equal parts are shaded.

O ――――――

- ## order

  Numbers can be ordered from least to greatest.

  28,539   31,707   33,450

  They can also be ordered from greatest to least.

  33,450   31,707   28,539

- ## outcome

  An outcome is the result in a probability experiment.

  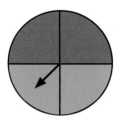

  There are two possible outcomes, green and red.

- ## outlier

  A number in a set of data that is much greater than or less than the other numbers in the data is an outlier.

Scores on an Art Paper	
Stem	**Leaves**
6	8
7	5 7
8	1 3 4
9	7

  6 | 8 = 68

  The stem-and-leaf plot for this set of data shows that the outlier is 97.

P

- ## place-value chart

  A place-value chart shows the value of each digit in a number.

Ten Thousands	Thousands	Hundreds	Tens	Ones
●●●	●●●●●●	●●●●	●	●●
3	6	4	1	2

  36,412 = 3 ten thousands + 6 thousands + 4 hundreds + 1 ten + 2 ones

- ## prime number

  A prime number has exactly two factors, 1 and itself.
  7 is a prime number: its factors are 1 and 7.

- ## probability

  Probability is a number from 0 to 1 that represents the chance or likelihood of an outcome occurring.

  $$Probability = \frac{Number\ of\ favorable\ outcomes}{Number\ of\ possible\ outcomes}$$

  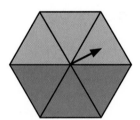

  The probability of landing on purple is $\frac{3}{6}$ or $\frac{1}{2}$.

- ## product

  A product is the answer to a multiplication problem.
  924 × 40 = 36,960
  The product of 924 and 40 is 36,960.

Q

- **quotient**

    A quotient is the answer to a division problem.
    $8,160 \div 6 = 1,360$
    The quotient of 8,160 divided by 6 is 1,360.

R

- **range**

    The range of a set of data is the difference between
    the greatest and the least number in the set.
    2   4   5   5   6   8   8   9   10   Range $= 10 - 2 = 8$

- **reasonable**

    $683 \times 4 = 2,732$
    683 is about 700.
    $700 \times 4 = 2,800$
    2,732 is close to 2,800. So the answer is reasonable.

- **regroup**

    One or more digits of a number may be regrouped when adding,
    subtracting, multiplying or dividing.
    When you regroup numbers, change:
    - 10 ones to 1 ten or 1 ten to 10 ones
    - 10 tens to 1 hundred or 1 hundred to 10 tens
    - 10 hundreds to 1 thousand or 1 thousand to 10 hundreds
    - 10 thousands to 1 ten thousand or 1 ten thousand to 10 thousands

- **remainder**

    A remainder is the number left over when a number cannot be
    divided evenly.
    $6,100 \div 8 = 762 \text{ R } 4$

- **round**

  A number can be rounded to the nearest ten or hundred by looking at the digit to the right of the tens or hundreds place. If it is less than 5, round down. If it is 5 or more than 5, round up.

  4,683 rounded to the nearest ten is 4,680.
  4,683 rounded to the nearest hundred is 4,700.

- **row**

  Data in a table is organized horizontally by rows.

  Popular Types of Food

Age group	Italian	Mexican	Chinese
Under 12	21	16	9
From 12 to 18	24	29	13
Over 18	35	26	28

  row

S

- **simplest form**

  A fraction in simplest form has no common factors other than 1 in the numerator and denominator.

  $\frac{3}{21}$ in simplest form is $\frac{1}{7}$.

- **standard form**

  The standard form of a number shows the number written with one digit for each place value.

  Forty-two thousand, eight hundred three in standard form is 42,803.

- ## stem-and-leaf plot

  A stem-and-leaf plot organizes data by place value.

Scores on an Art Paper	
Stem	**Leaves**
6	8
7	5 7
8	1 3 4
9	7

  6 | 8 = 68

T

- ## table

  A table organizes and presents data in rows and columns.

  Type of Fruit Bought

Fruit	Number
Oranges	3
Peaches	5
Strawberries	8

- ## tally chart

  A tally chart organizes data in groups of five.

  Type of Fruit Bought

Oranges	Peaches	Strawberries
///	/////	///// ///

- **ten thousand**

Ten Thousands	Thousands	Hundreds	Tens	Ones
	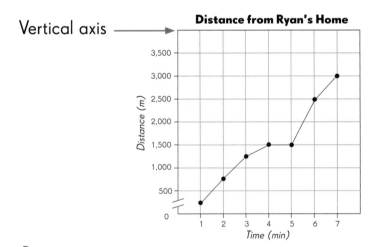			

10 thousands = 1 ten thousand

U

- **unlike fraction**

  Unlike fractions have different denominators.

  $\frac{2}{5}$ and $\frac{1}{4}$ are unlike fractions.

V

- **vertical axis**

  A vertical axis on a graph runs straight up and down.

Vertical axis ⟶

Distance from Ryan's Home

Distance (m) vs Time (min)

W

- **word form**

  73,816 in word form is seventy-three thousand, eight hundred sixteen.

Index

A

Acute angle, 90, 92–93, 97, 104; *WB 45–54, 57*

Addition
estimating sums, *See* Estimation
models, 224–226, 237–238, 250–251, 254, 259;
WB 137
with fractions, *See* Fractions
with mixed numbers, 230, 232, 250–251, 254, 259–260;
WB 155
sentence, *throughout. See for example* 32–35, 43, 66–67,
224–226, 243–254; *WB 15–17, 137–138*
with decimals, 4–79; *WB 21–26*

Algebraic thinking
bar models as variables, *See* Bar models
division sentences for real-world problems, *throughout. See*
for example 109, 111–113, 115, 119; *WB 59–62,*
91–92
formulas for area and perimeter, 152, 163, 166, 176,
183, *93–97*
multiplication sentences for real-world problems,
throughout. See for example 109, 110, 113, 115,
116, 119; *WB 59–62, 91–92*
number sentences with missing terms or symbols,
throughout. See for example 11, 13, 25, 33–39, 45,
53; *WB 5–6, 21–22, 41–42, 44*
patterns, 6, 8, 16, 19; *26–30, 34, 52; WB 2, 9, 10, 11,*
32, 36, 10, 12
properties of multiplication, *See* Multiplication
proportional reasoning, *See* Proportional reasoning

Angle(s)
acute, **90**, 92–93, 97, 104; *WB 48, 53*
definition of, 81, 83; *WB 45–50*
drawing, 94–104; *WB 51-54*
estimating, 82–84, 91; *WB 49*
measuring, 88–93; *WB 47, 49–50*
naming of, 83–84, 85–86, 93 ,95; *WB 45–46,*
obtuse, **90**–93, 97, 103–104; *WB 48, 53*
right, 82, 84, 88, 100; *WB 55–56*
straight, **95**
and turns, 98–102, 104; *WB 55–56*

Area
estimating, 158, 162, 184, 186, 193; *WB 97*
of a composite figure, 170–175, 178–187, 193; *WB*
109–110
of a rectangle, 152–155, 160–161, 166–169, 176,
178, 180–182, 184–185, 190, 191; *WB 93–97,*
103–106, 111–116
of a square, 154–155, 157, 161, 169, 190; *WB 94–95,*
96–99, 103–105

Assessment
Cumulative Review, *WB 35–40, 83–92, 171–180, 37–44,*
87–92, 147–154
Mid-Year Review, *WB 181–193*
End-of-Year Review, *WB 155–168*

Average, *See* Mean

B

Bar graph, 146, 148–150
using, to make a table, 130–133, 156; *WB 70, 85*

Bar models
comparing sets, 109, 111–113, 115, 119, 205, 269;
WB 62, 66, 91–92, 121, 135–136
fraction of a set, 255–257, 262–266, 269;
WB 158–159
joining sets, 111–112, 115, 225, 250, 259, 268–269;
WB 62, 137
part-part-whole, 110–112, 115, 119, 204, 225, 228,
250, 252, 259–260, 268–269; *WB 62, 137, 139*
taking away sets 110–111, 115, 119, 204, 228, 252,
260, 268–269; *WB 62, 139*
three-step problems, 109–113, 115, 259–266;
WB 62, 91–92

C

Base (of a drawing triangle), 115

Calculator, *WB 14*

Certain outcome, **193**, *See also* Outcomes—likelihood of

Chapter Review/Test, *See* Review

Chapter Wrap Up, *See* Review

Chip models, 5–7, 9–10, 12, 77–79, 82, 86, 96–99

Choose an appropriate graph, 146–150; *WB 78*

Common multiples, **58**, 59, 61, 68; *WB 29, 33, 39*

Pages listed in regular type refer to Student Book A.
Pages in blue type refer to Student Book B.
Pages in *black italic* type refer to Workbook (WB) A pages.
Pages in *blue italic* type refer to Workbook (WB) B pages.
Pages in **boldface** type show where a term is introduced.

Lines
    symbol for, 85
    horizontal, 119–124; *WB 65–68*
    parallel, 106–108, 119–118, 199–120
    perpendicular, 106–108, 119–120
    of symmetry, 197–202, 208–212, 215–217;
        WB 123–124
    vertical, 119–124; *WB 65–68*

Line graph, **140**
    interpreting, 140–144, 150, 158; *WB 75–77, 79–80,
        89–90*
    making, 145
    reading, 140–144, 150, 158; *WB 75–77, 79–80,
        89–90*
    using, 140–144, 148–150, 158; *WB 75–77, 79–80,
        89–90*

Line plot, **176**, 178–182, 184–186, 207, 214; *WB 104,
    106–108, 124–126, 171, 177*

Line of symmetry, **197**–202, 208–212, 215–217;
    WB 123–124

Line symmetry, **197**–202, 208–212, 215–217;
    WB 123–124

Line segment
    parallel and perpendicular, 106, 109–118, 120–124;
        WB 61–67
    symbol for, 85; *WB 61–67*

Make predictions, 192–195, 197, 201–203, 209–210;
    WB 113–114, 129–130, 172, 177

Manipulatives
    chip models, 5–7, 9–10, 12, 77–79, 82, 86, 96–99
    classroom objects, 9, 17, 170–171, 192–194, 197,
        200, 202
    connecting cubes, 166, 196
    counters, 12
    drawing triangle, 112–116, 121, 124; *WB 63–64,
        66–67*
    fraction circles, 231, 240
    geoboards, 133, 135, 156, 168
    measuring tape, 39
    number cubes, 82, 246
    place-value blocks, 71–75, 77

protractor, 88–97, 102, 104; *WB 47–54*
straightedge, 111–118, 121–122, 124, *WB 63–64,
    66–67*
ruler, 106
spinners, 194–195, 198–199, 209; *WB 115*

Math Journal, *See* Communication

Mean, **165**, 166–173, 177, 181–183, 185–186,
    204–208, 212–213, 215, 218–219; *WB 93–100,
    107–112, 119–126, 132–133, 135–136, 171,
    176–177*

Measures of central tendency, 204, *See also* Mean, Median,
    Mode, and Range

Median, **174**, 175–177, 180, 183–186, 188–191,
    206–208, 218; *WB 101–104, 106, 109–112,
    122–128, 171–172, 178*

Mid-Year Review, *See* Assessment

Mental math, 70

Mixed numbers,
    addition with, 230, 232, 250–251, 254, 259–260;
        WB 155
    as decimals, 44–45, 47, 52; *WB 6, 17–18*
    definition of, 230; *WB 141*
    improper fractions and, 237–254; *WB 147–154,
        174–175*
    modeling, 230–232, 234–236, 243–244, 248,
        250–252; *WB 141–145, 169, 174*
    on a number line, 233–236, 245–247; *WB 144–146,
        150*
    subtraction with, 252–254, 260–262, 265; *WB 156*

Mode, 178, 179–180, 183–185, 188–191, 206–208,
    213–214, 218; *WB 101–104, 106, 109–112, 122–
    124, 127–128, 134, 171–172, 177–178*

Models
    abstract, *throughout. See for example,* 45, 78–82, 224,
        232, 234–241, 243–244, 248, 250–252; *WB 62,
        66, 137, 139*
    concrete, 166, 192–193, 224, 227, 230–231, 255;
        WB 144
    geoboard, 133, 135, 156, 168

Pages listed in regular type refer to Student Book A.
Pages in blue type refer to Student Book B.
Pages in *black italic* type refer to Workbook (WB) A pages.
Pages in *blue italic* type refer to Workbook (WB) B pages.
Pages in **boldface** type show where a term is introduced.

with mixed numbers, *See* Mixed numbers
models, 227–229, 252–254, 260; *WB 139*
sentence, *throughout. See for example* 33–35, 41, 43,
   66–67; *WB 15–17, 139–140*

Symmetry, 194–217; *WB 123–129*

Photo Credits

Blank

Blank

Blank

Blank

Blank